Overcoming Anger for Couples

Navigating anger and conflict in relationships: A guide to understanding, communication, and coping strategies for couples to build a stronger relationship.

Emotion Tutor

Contents

Chapter 1

INTRODUCTION

Are you experiencing difficulties controlling your anger and resolving conflicts as a couple? It's common to feel angry in the moment, but when these emotions accumulate over time. Many women struggle to express their needs and desires, either by remaining silent or speaking out in anger, whereas men often resort to passive-aggressive behavior to achieve their goals. It's not the responsibility of one person to manage the emotions of the other, and anger can be effectively utilized as a means of communication to convey what needs to be improved. If partners communicate assertively instead of resorting to aggressive or passive-aggressive behaviors, it will contribute to a healthier relationship.

Learning how to deal with anger effectively and work through conflict with your partner will increase the amount of trust between you both. It's easy to get stuck in negative thought patterns that prevent you from expressing your true feelings and communicating openly with each other. As a result, resentment may build up over time until it reaches a boiling point where one or both explode in anger. There are no set guidelines for resolving conflicts, however, this guide will provide you with insights on how to handle various situations and build stronger and more positive relationships. By understanding and applying these principles, you can work towards creating a healthier and more fulfilling relationship.

This book offers helpful tools to communicate better with your partner by identifying methods that work for you. It also provides a deeper understanding of how both partners may contribute to the problem, not just one side or the other. You'll be able to understand why each of you acts the way you do when it comes to anger and how you can eventually change your behavior to resolve the conflict. When both partners contribute towards a solution, you're more likely to find one that works for both of you instead of fighting over something that only benefits one person or perhaps no one. Partners who can identify their issues and their partner can find a solution much more quickly than two people who keep pointing fingers at each other without finding solutions to where things went wrong.

A relationship is supposed to provide safety and comfort for both partners through mutual respect, trust, and love. It's easy for resentment to build up and minor issues to overwhelm the bigger ones if the couple can't find a way to address them. The truth is that anger is a natural reaction to feeling hurt or being in an uncomfortable situation, so learning how to deal with it can help you both.

Understanding what makes you angry and how to communicate healthily can strengthen your relationship. "Anger management" is often used to control how one expresses anger, but that's only one piece of the puzzle. If one partner wants things to change, but the other partner refuses, nothing will change, and resentment will continue to build. In the same way that anger needs an outlet, the conflict also needs the resolution to find happiness in your relationship.

Often anger and conflict between couples are not really about whether one person is wrong or right but rather about sharing responsibility for the problem. A strong relationship needs respect and trust from both partners, who are very involved in both sides of the argument to keep it from crumbling. And while no one learns a lesson by being told they were wrong or having their feelings hurt, it's important to show understanding and compassion when you hear someone else express their true feelings.

These aren't necessarily easy concepts to learn because we all struggle with issues that may be more powerful than our relationship. It's important to realize that anger can be destructive to your relationship, and if you're only trying to change your partner, you'll likely never find a solution. Learning to control anger is a good start, but managing conflict will make for a healthy relationship. It starts with truly understanding each other and accepting the power struggles that may lead to one person becoming angry or resentful.

Instead of seeing it as an attack, see it as a way of learning about what needs to change within you or your partner. It's essential not to take things personally because no one wants to feel attacked when their partner expresses their feelings in their way. The purpose of this book is to provide tools used by a wide variety of couples to create stronger relationships rather than just looking at anger as a problem. We will examine how anger arises and relates to conflict, communication, and control. We will also discuss the importance of managing anger in relationships for stronger bonds, the adverse effects of unresolved anger on communication, trust, and intimacy, the impact of anger on both partners' physical and mental health, and the benefits of healthy anger management.

Improved communication, increased empathy and understanding, reduced stress and tension, strategies for identifying triggers and coping mechanisms for anger include deep breathing, mindfulness, setting boundaries, techniques for constructive conflict resolution, and the role of forgiveness in fostering a positive and healthy relationship. All these topics will be covered in the book, allowing you to understand how anger works within relationships and how it can be managed effectively to prevent or reduce conflict.

When you feel like your relationship is falling apart, it's easy to believe that you're powerless to create changes. You may be tempted to give up and call it quits but giving up is just going from one unhealthy situation into another because now you're alone. Taking control of your thoughts and actions can bring change into your life instead of waiting for someone else to fix things for you. To improve a relationship, you must take an inventory of what's not working and find solutions that meet your needs. Most women are used to being the fixer, but you can't fix a situation if you don't know what's wrong with it in the first place. Men often hide their feelings and don't want to look weak by sharing their feelings. Both partners need to make space in their lives to talk about what's bothering them; otherwise, it will worsen over time.

Understanding your thoughts and feelings is critical to successful communication with your partner because it will enable you to listen attentively without jumping to conclusions or reacting defensively. It's easy to feel sometimes attacked when you're trying to communicate with your partner, and it's essential that both people feel respected and safe. It's also vital for both of you to understand what is upsetting the other person and then meet them in the middle by finding a solution that works. If there's a will to improve things, you'll find a way to get there. That's a powerful statement that takes some time to sink in. Sometimes people are so distraught over the current state of their relationship that they're tempted to give up, but it can be done if both partners are committed to making it work again.

When you both have strong wills and set clear boundaries, it will be easier for you to communicate more effectively and develop ways to improve things. You may not always agree on everything, but by listening actively and testing your assumptions about your partner, you'll be able to work together on finding solutions that work for both of you. If problems are left unresolved, then frustration, anger, and resentment will build up until one day, an argument will erupt between the two people in the relationship. That's not the kind of communication you should be looking forward to because that only leads to more arguing, fighting, and potential physical or emotional abuse.

Transform Your Relationship: A Comprehensive Guide to Anger Management for Couples

The common types of anger include passive, aggressive, and assertive bitterness. Which one you experience depends on the situation and how much anger you can manage. Your thoughts determine your emotions, but emotions also assess your thoughts. If you successfully manage your anger, shift your thinking, and consider a different perspective will be more accessible when things get complicated. That strengthens your relationship because no argument or conflict will be sustained if both people are committed to making things work for them. Anger causes include unmet expectations, communication breakdowns, or past traumas. It is important to acknowledge because that's when you will better understand why you're feeling the way you do. It's possible to feel angry even if you have no reason to feel that way, but something else is likely bothering you. The potential consequences of untreated anger in relationships will be devastating. It will lead to emotional and physical abuse, decreased intimacy, and an increased likelihood of separation or divorce.

By learning to manage your anger, you can avoid that and focus on your partner's needs instead of your own. Emotions will always influence our thoughts, but you will have to choose how you respond to them. That will determine the kind of person you are, and it will also select the type of man or woman you attract into your life. Anger is normal, but it is destructive if not managed correctly. Learning how to communicate healthily is essential because both people need to feel safe and respected within the relationship for it to work. No one wants to be around someone who yells at them all the time or refuses to listen when they try to speak.

Today, people are more likely to express their anger in controlled ways, whether in aggression outbursts or significant changes in attitude. Couples are expected to communicate with each other using anger to react to difficult situations instead of discovering why they are angry and working together to find solutions. When anger is used to express frustration, it leads to other issues, such as subtle hostility and conflict. It's important to remember that everyone has some anger issues, but it's also essential to manage them effectively and prevent them from escalating. Anger management in relationships isn't a quick fix; it takes time and effort to get there. Being angry is part of being human, but it damages your life when you become chronically mad.

Chapter 2

ANGER UNPACKED

A nger can be an intimidating emotion at times, if you are unable to identify the root causes of your anger, it can become more challenging to deal with in a relationship. This is why it is important to comprehend the essence of anger and to develop the skills to work effectively with your partner.

UNDERSTANDING ANGER

Anger is a feeling or behavior that is aggressive, and it can be expressed in several ways. Anger may be exhibited at either a behavioral level or as a feeling. There are many different forms of anger, each corresponding to another type of emotion or the source of pain. If something triggers your anger, you are face-to-face with a stronger emotion. It's like when something happens to upset your sense of peace and calm. In this case, you experience anger because there is a threat to the state of your peacefulness. When there is no immediate threat, your anger subsides over time. This happens when there isn't an immediate problem causing your irritation. As long as the threat goes away, the hostility goes away with it. When a threat remains, unaddressed anger will remain in our system until we address it or learn how to manage it.

Anger is a natural emotion. It's how we defend ourselves when confronted with something threatening to us. This includes threats to our physical well-being and our sense of security. A danger can trigger anger, from minor things to brutal events. Couples, like people in general, experience both types of threats. However, anger becomes an issue for many couples because of how they handle it. Anger can also be a big part of our everyday life. It's how we express our feelings and how we communicate with one another. Anger is the essence of communication because it's the feeling that connects us all.

The feelings and emotions within anger cause us to act in specific ways. When you feel angry, for example, you may experience a desire to fight back or lash out in some fashion. This is what we often call aggressive behavior, which is often misunderstood by both ourselves and others as bad, but it's simply natural. There are many different components of anger and how they interact to create an angry disposition. At times you will experience the following components in anger; understanding each will help you build a stronger relationship.

Emotional response

Emotions are the experience that accompanies anger. This includes anger-related emotions like fear, sadness, and guilt. Emotions are universal experiences that are hardwired into our nervous system. When you experience an emotion, you can't help but feel it without appearing to be a lunatic. Your biology predisposes you to feel certain emotions, and your psychology and upbringing influence how these emotions develop.

Because of this, we may not recognize or understand different types of emotions when they arise during an angry experience because they essentially feel familiar, even if they're unfamiliar to us in some way. Emotions tell us what we need to be healthy and happy (confidence, security, love).

Emotions play a critical role in anger as they serve as signals that alert us to potential danger and activate our fight-or-flight response. This response prepares us to take action, whether it be to confront a threat or to flee from it. Emotions are therefore an important component of our survival mechanism and help us respond quickly and effectively to perceived dangers.

Mental response

Our cognitive responses are our thoughts, beliefs, and attitudes related to the anger experience in some form or another. It's how we interpret the situation that anger presents us with and how we make sense of it to understand why it's happening.

Mental responses are often associated with emotions, as they exist between our feelings and attitudes toward certain situations. Cognitive responses also help explain why people respond differently from one another, even if there is a shared experience among them.

Without a theoretical framework, mental responses to anger are hard to identify and understand. Anger has different meanings for different people in different situations, as every situation defines its unique meaning.

Body response

The physical response is the energetic activity we engage in during angry experiences. The body's physical expression of anger usually consists of a fight-or-flight response, but this isn't always the case. Not all people with anger experience this at all times concerning the situation when they experience it.

It also involves overreaction and emotional outbursts that express a rampant state of rage or excitement (anger per se). We often experience our emotions through the body, which is most apparent when we experience anger.

When you feel angry, you have no control over it. Your body reacts to your emotions and produces physical changes that indicate that you are feeling something. You cannot avoid feeling what you feel, so part of your responsibility lies in expressing your anger.

Emotions influence how they express themselves when a situation calls for them to express themselves in a particular way: through our body responses to an angry experience. For example, anger expressed through physical aggression and aggression expressed through emotional outbursts are both forms of aggressive behavior that can be expressed in a healthy or unhealthy way.

Constructive and destructive actions

If you're angry, you can use productive activities that help you resolve the situation and healthily channel your anger. Or you can engage in destructive actions that harm yourself, the people involved with the situation, or both.

Constructive actions are means through which we transform our anger into something that benefits us. They involve expressing our emotions healthy, such as having a good cry or giving yourself space to process what happened without being self-destructive or destructive to others.

Physical Anger and Psychological Changes

The physiological changes during an angry experience include increased heart rate, blood pressure, breathing rate, perspiration, and muscle tension. These changes are more pronounced in a chronic or intense anger situation. Psychological changes typically occur during an angry experience, including feelings of sadness, disbelief, superiority, and frustration that all make up the clash within your mind.

Physically, you experience anger through the body. This is when you engage in physical aggression to express your rage or when your body moves according to your emotion (clenching hands, holding back tears). However, this doesn't mean we can't have peace while experiencing this phase. Our mind influences our physical reactions, like our heart rate increasing while we are angry, because it attempts to match the demands of our body response.

When our bodies react to an angry experience in this way, it's called our fight-or-flight response. This response results from stress hormones like epinephrine and cortisol rising when faced with a stressful situation. It's meant to prepare us for physical activity and often responds in anger to protect us from harm or any other threat we may face.

Once again, these physiological changes can also happen without psychological reactions. Very stressed people may experience physiological changes that require no psychological response, even though they have an angry experience. This is not to say that there is no connection between the physical and mental responses of anger.

Sometimes, people's physical reactions are a byproduct of their thinking. Feeling sad or angry and developing anger may be related because it's part of a continuum of thoughts and emotions that occur during an angry experience.

TYPES OF ANGER

There are many different types of anger, and each type is experienced differently. Some people become anxious when they are angry; others experience significant distress. People experience anger in different ways or diffuse anger, but the most common way is anger focused on a person or thing.

People can experience anger in various ways: directed at a person or people, at an object such as a weapon, animal, or even a tree. This can be either physical aggression (hitting and slapping), verbal aggression (saying mean things), or non-physical aggression (withdrawing from relationships, destroying things)

Different people experience and express their anger in different ways. They may be experiencing the same emotion simultaneously through various channels of expression. Although all people experience anger, the way it displays is unique to each individual.

Some types of anger are expressed through repressed anger, passive-aggressive, and explosive anger. These are all ways in which people use different types. People can also experience anger subtly, such as by being angry with themselves. This type of anger is generally expressed through self-destructive or self-defeating behaviors.

Here are some types of anger that cause problems:

1. Passive anger

Passive anger means that the anger is not expressed but remains inside and is expressed later. This type has been a problem for couples unaware that anger is always part of a relationship; most people experience angry feelings at one point or another. Passive anger can destroy your relationship when it goes unchecked because it can become directed toward you and your children.

Passive anger is usually expressed in a non-verbal manner; it doesn't have to be screamed or shouted. People might roll their eyes and scowl while stewing over an incident between them and their partner. The passive-angry person may also feel a sense of being controlled. When you try to get your point across, the angry individual becomes silent and is often sarcastic in response to what you have to say. This can make the passive angry person feel that they are being put down or controlled by you.

Passive anger is a form of behavior that can be just as damaging to a relationship as explosive anger. One characteristic of passive anger is stonewalling, which is when your partner completely ignores your presence and refuses to communicate. This can be just as harmful as being aggressive and can cause tension in your relationship. Another characteristic of passive anger is withholding affection. If your partner is suspicious of being taken advantage of, they may withhold affection, which can make it difficult for you to feel close to them. This causes a sense of disconnection between partners.

Many people may be reluctant to praise or express appreciation for something good that has happened, which can lead to a relationship where compliments and praise are withheld. This is hurtful and causes a sense of disconnection between partners. When your partner constantly judges you, it can create feelings of inadequacy and low self-esteem. It can make you feel as if you are never good enough and that your partner is constantly finding fault with you. This constant criticism can erode your confidence and make you feel unsure of yourself.

Additionally, constant judgment can create a sense of feeling unloved. When someone judges you, it can feel as if they are attacking you and not accepting you for who you are. This can lead to a feeling of disconnection and distance in the relationship, which can be harmful and make it difficult to maintain a strong and loving bond. But it is important to remember that everyone has their own unique qualities and strengths, and it is not healthy for someone to make you feel inadequate. If your partner's constant judgment is causing harm to the relationship, it may be necessary to discuss the issue and find a resolution that works for both partners. With effort and communication, it is possible to overcome this form of passive anger and maintain a strong and loving relationship.

2. Explosive Anger

Explosive anger in couples is a type of anger that is characterized by sudden and intense outbursts that can be verbal or physical. This type of anger is often triggered by a perceived threat or challenge to the individual's sense of control or power in the relationship.

Examples of explosive anger in couples might include shouting, name-calling, and physical attacks. For example, one partner might throw objects or physically assault the other partner during an argument. Another example might include a partner who explodes with anger and start shouting and using offensive language when they feel that their authority or control in the relationship is being challenged.

In some cases, explosive anger can be a result of a personal history of abuse, fear of being powerless, or trust issues. Individuals who have experienced trauma or abuse in their past may be particularly prone to explosive anger as a way of coping with these experiences. This type of anger can also stem from a lack of trust in the relationship, causing the individual to feel threatened and leading to an explosive outburst.

Explosive anger can have a significant impact on the relationship, causing emotional stress and strain for both partners. It is important for couples to address and manage this behavior in order to maintain a healthy and positive relationship. One can help your partner better express their rage by encouraging them to express their feelings in a healthy manner that does not involve physical attacks or threats of physical harm.

If you or your partner is experiencing explosive anger, you may be familiar with some of the common forms it takes, such as threats to leave the relationship. This type of behavior can stem from a feeling of helplessness and can be used to intimidate the other partner. It is important to recognize when this type of behavior becomes manipulative and to take steps to protect yourself from fear and intimidation.

Verbal abuse, such as name-calling, is also a common form of explosive anger in relationships. Also, Physical abuse is another devastating form of explosive anger and can have serious consequences for both partners. If you or your partner is struggling with control in your relationship, it is important to seek help before it escalates to physical violence. Remember that violence is never an acceptable solution and can cause permanent damage to your relationship and those involved.

3. Passive-aggressive anger

Passive-aggressive anger is often displayed in a more indirect or covert manner. It may involve non-verbal cues, such as slumping or shutting down, or passive resistance, such as refusing to participate or ignoring requests. People who experience passive-aggressive anger may feel a range of negative emotions, such as guilt, shame, and helplessness.

Passive-aggressive behavior in romantic relationships can take many forms and can be damaging to the relationship if not addressed. One common example of passive aggression is the silent treatment, where a partner refuses to communicate or acknowledge the other's presence. Sarcasm is another form of passive-aggression, where a partner may make snide or cutting remarks in a seemingly joking manner. The "forgetful" act is when a partner pretends to forget important tasks or requests made by their partner, and the blame game involves constantly blaming the partner for problems but avoiding direct confrontation.

Another form of passive-aggression is the martyr act, where a partner may pretend to be the victim and overdo it with the "poor me" attitude. Indirect criticism involves making subtle or indirect comments about a partner's behavior or choices that are meant to hurt or criticize. Sabotage, where a partner deliberately hinders the other's efforts or goals without openly expressing anger or frustration, is another form of passive-aggression. Withholding affection, where a partner refuses to show affection or intimacy as a form of punishment, is another example.

This type of anger can be directed either toward oneself or towards others and can take the form of either passive or aggressive behavior. Passive aggression is often considered covert aggression because it is expressed in a less obvious manner, such as providing incorrect information or refusing to comply with requests. Passive-aggression can be a toxic pattern of behavior that undermines trust, communication, and intimacy in a relationship. It can leave both partners feeling frustrated, hurt, and resentful.

4. Chronic anger

Chronic anger refers to a persistent and long-lasting state of anger that has the potential to negatively impact a person's physical and emotional well-being. Chronic anger can stem from deep-seated resentment, or feelings of injustice, or may even be a symptom of depression. When anger is not properly managed and remains in a chronic state, it can lead to serious health consequences such as depression, poor physical health, and in severe cases, death.

In a relationship, chronic anger can be particularly damaging. When one partner is constantly angry, it can create an atmosphere of tension and mistrust, leading to a breakdown in communication and intimacy. Chronic anger in a relationship may manifest as persistent resentment towards one's partner, an inability to trust them, and a deep sadness or hopelessness that results in unhappiness in the relationship.

Common symptoms of this type of chronic anger can be the person appearing angry most of the time, negative and pessimistic behavior, a decline in creativity, and feelings of resentment that lead to an inability to trust your partner. When people are unable to express their anger, it can build up inside them, leading to feelings of resentment that only serve to further fuel their anger.

CAUSES OF ANGER

1. Poor communication

As you know communication is a critical factor in any relationship; if it is lacking, it will result in a lack of understanding and empathy. If one person in a relationship has chronic anger issues, they may not communicate with their partner because they are not understood. When one believes they have to repeat themselves repeatedly and constantly, this can lead to a loss of respect for their partner. This can cause the angry person to resent their partner, likely resulting in a conflict.

2. Unmet Expectations

When one person in the relationship expects that they want to be fulfilled, and their partner isn't open to doing this, this can result in anger. If the angry person feels they are not being respected, they will become angry and may use passive-aggressive aggression.

Many people have expectations about how a relationship should be, and these may differ from their partner's expectations. For example, a person may want to be affectionate and desired, but their partner is not receptive to this. This can end up ruining the relationship because anger can build up if you are unhappy with the way your partner acts in their relationship with you.

3. Lack of trust

If one person in a relationship doesn't trust the other, this is likely to result in anger and resentment. Trust is essential to any relationship, and repeated broken promises can destroy it. If you are in a relationship where your trust has been misplaced, you will have a lowered sense of respect for your partner, leading to long-term feelings of anger. When people fear that they may lose their partner and feel concerned about their relationship's safety and security, it can lead to chronic anger.

4. Feeling threatened

If one person feels that they are being threatened, then it can result in anger. For example, suppose your partner is talking to someone who makes you feel uncomfortable, or they won't tell you about a meeting they are attending, and you feel your sense of trust has been violated. If left unchecked, this situation can lead to a buildup of anger within you.

5. Financial Problems

Financial problems can also result in anger. If one person feels that their partner is spending too much money on themselves and is entitled to get all the benefits they want, this will result in anger. People are often frustrated when they know their partner isn't honest with them about spending. To control your anger, you will need to be as honest as possible with your partner and work out a system where you can manage finances, so it doesn't result in an argument.

If one person is struggling financially, they may be relying on their partner to help them with financial problems that prevent them from affording things they need or want.

6. Infidelity

Infidelity is a destructive and painful experience that can result in extreme anger. If one person finds out their partner has been unfaithful to them, it can lead to the person experiencing passionate rage.

Infidelity can lead to anger in the relationship, often due to feelings of betrayal and loss. When someone else is attracted to your partner inappropriately, this can result in anger. If your partner is unfaithful, you need to consider whether you can trust them again or if they are likely to be unfaithful. This can result in a feeling of distrust, which you may feel toward your partner. If you think your partner is cheating, you will find it difficult to trust them again, leading to chronic anger.

When you are in a relationship, it is vital to recognize your anger and what is causing it. You need to understand the root cause of your anger, and if you are dealing with a chronic state of anger, you will need to do something about it before it destroys your relationship. If you often feel angry towards your partner, you need to talk to them about how they make you feel.

HOW PAST EXPERIENCES AND CHILDHOOD CAN INFLUENCE ANGER IN ADULTHOOD?

If an individual is exposed to unpredictable, inconsistent parenting as a child, they are likely to develop anger as an adult. The person will be unable to handle stress in their adult life because they could not learn how to cope with it in childhood.

We have all had different experiences in life, and how we cumulate these experiences can establish how we deal with problems and frustrations in our adult life. It is important to remember that people can deal with their anger differently, depending on their unique situations and circumstances. We may see a friend or family member get angry in a situation, and we may think they are overreacting. Still, it's important to remember that they have experienced different things in their lifetime. Some people have never been taught how to manage their anger, which can lead to anger issues and an angry personality.

It is essential to understand how your anger behavior developed, as this can help you to manage it. What if you were exposed to unpredictable and inconsistent parenting as a child; in that case, you may feel a lot of anger toward your parents, but you need to understand that they had no idea what they were doing and didn't realize their negative impact on you. When people feel hurt during childhood or adolescence (or at any time in their adult life), it can lead to long-term anger because their expectations have been violated or rejected.

Impact of childhood trauma and unresolved issues on anger in adulthood:

Trauma can play an essential role in the development of an angry personality. When someone has experienced traumatic experiences that have stuck with them from childhood, they will have to deal with those issues as adults. If you are someone who has experienced trauma as a child and it hasn't been dealt with, then this will result in anger problems and an angry personality.

People who cannot cope with their trauma are at a high risk of developing anger issues. We all experience trauma at some point, and when it happens, we must remember that this is not our fault or our responsibility.

Here are some of the effects of childhood trauma and unresolved issues on anger in adulthood:

1. Personality and Character Issues

People with personality and character issues can find it difficult to get angry appropriately. They might have aggressive tendencies, and they may take the anger out on others, or they might become angry towards themselves. If one person has unresolved childhood problems and psychological issues, this can result in personality flaws or character problems.

When people recognize that their anger is out of control and affecting their life, it is essential to accept that you will need to address your issues. You can't expect your anger problems to disappear magically, but you can learn how to manage them better. It's important to remember that you don't have control over your anger, and it's not always something you can change, but you can learn strategies to help you manage your emotions well.

2. Lack of Self-Confidence

If people lack self-confidence and are always angry, they are more likely to take more extreme actions to feel validated in their actions. This will lead them to a whole life of destructive behavior, and they may neglect things that would usually be seen as essential goals or dreams they want to achieve. When people lack self-confidence, they may blame others for their problems, leading to anger problems. They may feel like their self-esteem has been taken away from them, and they need to learn that it's not their fault and it's important to remember that they are entitled to respect.

When you lack self-confidence, working on your self-esteem and self-image is essential. You can quickly improve your confidence by looking in the mirror every morning and repeating three positive aspects about yourself. Doing this will help you develop a more positive outlook and ignore negative things people have said about you. You can also improve your confidence by acknowledging good things about yourself. If you feel bad about yourself, you should start to take pride in the good things. This will increase your self-confidence and help you be more confident in handling your anger.

3. Impulsive Behaviors

Impulsive behaviors can result from childhood trauma because people who were abused as a child may develop emotional issues and out-of-control impulses. They may have intense emotions, leading to impulsive actions and adding to their violent tendencies. The lack of self-control and impulse control can result in people displaying anger problems when stressed and frustrated. They may lash out at people because they need to feel something; they may hurt a loved one on accident or be reckless with their actions.

4. Stuck in Negative Patterns of Thinking

If you have a set of negative patterns of thinking, then this can result in delayed emotional processing, leading to an angry personality. When you have negative ways of thinking, then it's likely that you will see the world as threatening and dangerous, which can make it difficult for you to cope with stress in life. Negative thinking patterns can result in angry outbursts, especially when people are stressed. They may have a reaction that goes against what they think they should be doing, and this will lead to them acting aggressively. This may happen when people are under stress, or it may happen whether they are under pressure or not.

5. Self-Blame

Self-blame is when people blame themselves for their anger problems, especially if they believe they are terrible people because of them. This can result in people becoming depressed, and this can lead to feelings of anger. People who feel evil for being angry will have difficulty coping with their emotions and dealing with situations that may trigger negative emotions. This is a type of psychological projection; this means that you are blaming yourself for something when you have done nothing wrong. This can make people feel incredibly guilty about their actions, and they may feel like they deserve to be punished for something they have done.

6. Impaired Physical Health

How you treat your body significantly impacts how it functions and interacts with the world around you. If your body is always angry, then there is a good chance that it's suffering from various negative health issues as well as emotional and psychological problems. The way we interact with our environment has an impact on our physical health and disease prevention. If we feel anger is born out of negative emotions, our bodies will mirror this, resulting in physical ailments.

If you have a poor quality of life and feel it's not worth living, you will have difficulty coping with your anger issues. This can lead to physical health issues such as anxiety or serious illnesses, resulting in lower self-esteem and depression.

THE EFFECTS OF ANGER ON RELATIONSHIPS

When you're in a relationship, and your anger problems start to affect your relationships, you need to address them, or your relationship will suffer. There are a few ways that anger can affect relationships, and you need to know how to deal with this if you want to keep the relationship healthy and active in a positive way.

Some of the ways that anger can affect relationships are:

1. Decreased intimacy

Decreased intimacy as a result of anger is a common issue in many relationships. When anger is present, it can lead to feelings of defensiveness and resentment, which can cause partners to distance themselves from one another. This distance can then lead to decreased physical and emotional intimacy, as partners may be less likely to engage in affectionate behaviors or have deep, vulnerable conversations.

This lack of intimacy has a significant impact on the health and happiness of a relationship. It can cause partners to feel lonely and unsupported, leading to a decline in overall relationship satisfaction. If left unaddressed, the decreased intimacy may also lead to feelings of boredom and a lack of passion in the relationship, which makes it difficult for partners to maintain a strong emotional connection.

2. Communication breakdown

When your anger issues make you angry and lash out at others, it is difficult for your partner to talk to you about their feelings. This is because the fear of the conflict escalates into a full-blown argument. If you have anger issues, then it's likely that you will struggle to communicate with others. Communication is one of the most important aspects of a relationship if it works properly and keeps your relationship healthy and happy. People with anger problems may find they cannot communicate their feelings with their partner healthily.

If you struggle to communicate with others and can't talk about your feelings and emotions, then there is a high chance that you will be unable to open up to your partner about what's going on for you. This may make them feel like something is wrong with them or they aren't necessary for your life. Whether the problem is anger related or not, this will likely result in poor communication skills between the couple.

3. Increased likelihood of physical and emotional abuse

There may be times when your anger issues lead you to abuse your partner or others. When this happens, it makes it difficult for you to recognize physically and emotionally abusive behavior and will result in the abuse going unchecked.

You may feel that you are justified in acting out on people because of how you feel angry, and this makes them think that they have done something wrong when they have not. There is a high chance that the person you abuse will be afraid of a full-blown physical attack, which may prevent them from speaking out against the abuse they are receiving. This will create an unhealthy environment where the abuser feels justified in their behavior, and the victim may think they deserve to be abused.

4. Decreased relationship satisfaction

The way you deal with your issues will have a significant impact on the satisfaction of your relationship. If you avoid dealing with your anger correctly, then it's likely that you will start to feel unhappy with this behavior and think that something needs to change. This causes resentment towards your partner and may eventually lead to the breakdown of the relationship.

5. Lead to divorce or health issues

Some people who struggle with anger issues reach a point where they feel they cannot cope and their feelings of anger are too much to handle. This results in their partner leaving the relationship and feeling that they cannot live with the person anymore. If the partner leaves the relationship, this will lead to problems within it and damages the person who left.

If you live your life dealing with anger issues, there is a high chance that you will resent your partner when they leave you because of your behavior. If you work on addressing your anger issues and learning to control them, you will feel more relaxed in front of your partner, and it will be easier for you to communicate with them. If you are happy and relaxed, this will allow you to communicate better and in turn will improve your relationships. You can also ensure that the relationship is going in a way that makes both of you happy, rather than just one person.

HOW ANGER CAN ALSO HAVE POSITIVE EFFECTS IF EXPRESSED IN HEALTHY WAYS?

There are also instances where anger can help improve your relationships, as long as you express it correctly. This can be from a simple verbal reaction to someone who has been a bully or an incident that has made you feel uncomfortable or upset. If you have anger issues, it might be difficult for you to express these feelings because of how angry you become, but this doesn't mean that these feelings cannot be expressed.

It's essential for people who struggle with their anger issues to realize that there are ways of expressing themselves without lashing out at others. If they do not get rid of their anger issues, they should try avoiding lashing out at others and instead use healthy ways to express their emotions. These healthy ways include:

1. Increased assertiveness

Many angry people may experience a loss of control, making them lash out at others aggressively. If you want to express your anger healthily, you should find ways to gain control over it. This can mean speaking honestly with others or finding another outlet for your emotions. Being assertive can make getting what you want and need more accessible, even in a relationship.

If you have no control over your anger, you will likely do things you regret later. For example, if your partner asks for some money and you get angry instead of giving it to them, then this may lead to arguments.

2. Improved communication

If you are angry with your partner, then they may not be able to understand why you're angry or what it is that has upset you. This can cause many problems within the relationship, as the two of you will not know how to connect and resolve an issue. Communicating appropriately is necessary for a healthy relationship if you struggle with anger issues.

Establishing communication between the two of you is necessary for an effective relationship because it allows you to resolve problems that have arisen and help improve relationships. When communicating with your partner, it is important to be calm and avoid becoming defensive or aggressive. This creates a safe and non-threatening environment that allows both partners to express their thoughts and feelings openly and honestly. Additionally, active listening is key, which means paying attention to what your partner is saying and truly understanding their perspective. This fosters mutual respect and can help to resolve conflicts and build a stronger relationship.

3. Increased intimacy

Being in close contact with someone is essential for any successful relationship. This can be through simple gestures such as touching the arm or sitting close to your partner. People with anger issues may not feel comfortable getting close to others, especially if they get angry when they do.

If you're struggling with anger issues, you may feel that intimacy will cause you to lash out at someone else and end up being aggressive with them. Understandably, people dealing with anger might think this is the case, but this doesn't have to be. Getting close to others doesn't mean you will lash out at them and be aggressive.

If you work on overcoming your anger issues, you should feel more comfortable with intimacy and being in close contact with someone else. This will allow you to get close to others and feel healthier and happier within your relationship.

4. Increased trust

When people deal with anger issues, they may not believe that their partner is trustworthy or reliable when handling problems in the relationship. Domestic violence usually occurs when people don't trust their partners or when there are feelings of jealousy and resentment within the relationship. If you are dealing with these feelings yourself, then it's likely that your partner feels the same way about you too.

Trusting those around you and believing they can be counted on is essential. If you don't believe this about your partner, then this may cause problems in the relationship. However, if you are in a relationship where one person has anger issues, this will lead to many conflicts. If you struggle with anger issues, it can affect your relationship with your partner and cause conflict between you. This can result from one partner not trusting the other and lashing out at them when they make mistakes or do not take responsibility for actions that were their fault.

5. Increased respect

Respect can be essential to any relationship, no matter how close you are to someone. If you have anger issues, this can be affected by how you speak to your partner and handle situations in the relationship. A lack of respect within a relationship can cause many issues that may result in arguments or the end of the relationship altogether. Understanding your partner's goals, values, and interests will help improve your relationship and help you overcome any problems that may arise from handling anger issues.

6. Improved communication skills

With improved communication skills, resolving conflicts without feeling angry or frustrated at another person will be much easier, which can often lead to domestic violence incidents in relationships. Maintaining healthy communication and solving conflicts will be more challenging if you struggle with anger issues.

7. Increased emotional control

This can be achieved through being able to show respect to your partner, as well as discovering how they were feeling at the time of a conflict. It's important to understand that you are doing this for your own sake and the sake of your relationship. Anger issues within a relationship can make resolving conflict difficult and damage the relationship in some way or another. Work on developing communication skills that allow you to express yourself without getting angry when talking with others and improve your emotional control by identifying when you have a problem within your relationships and what you need to do about it.

8. Improved decision-making and problem-solving skills

If you struggle with anger issues, this will be extremely difficult for you to do. You'll be more likely to lash out at others and not listen when they are speaking. This will cause many problems within the relationship, as the two of you will not be able to resolve issues together in a healthy manner when it's so easy for you to fly off the handle at any given moment. Improving your decision-making skills can allow you to work through problems with your partner or other people without being angry or irritated, as this will help promote healthy relationships.

9. Greater impulse control and self-regulation

If you have anger issues, you likely lack impulse control when dealing with others around you and handling problems in your life. This should be worked on immediately, as it will help improve your relationship with others, including your significant other. This can be achieved by identifying situations where you feel angry or irritated and searching for ways of handling the situation healthily and constructively without lashing out at another person or yourself.

There are ways of expressing yourself without getting angry at others. As an individual, you may find that you become angry and upset with others at times. This is normal and doesn't mean that you are the wrong person or that someone else is being awful to you. If you have anger issues, this can be connected to how a certain situation or action can trigger people. Sometimes this connection becomes more robust and motivates you to lash out at others because it feels good or better than your usual self.

Expressing yourself without getting angry at others:

Take a different approach to certain situations. When you feel angry or upset, it is essential to understand that this is how you feel at that time and to take a different approach. If a situation doesn't make you feel good, think about another way of dealing with it, even if this means going along with something you know isn't right. Identify where the anger comes from and work on changing this area of your life. If there is an area in your life where you feel resentment against someone else or yourself, then think about how you could improve yourself in this area. Try and understand why you are feeling angry and find ways of improving so that things don't affect your relationship negatively any longer.

1.Discuss your feelings with others

If you struggle with anger issues, you need to speak with someone about your inner turmoil. Sometimes when we don't talk about our feelings, they can build up and cause issues later in life. Understanding where your problems lie and how to improve them can be highly beneficial in resolving most issues you might have within your relationships. If you feel angry, try and think about the situation in a different way. Sometimes we might be too focused on what we think when someone has upset us that we have no idea how to handle our anger at them. Seeing the situation differently can help you overcome your anger issues and not lose your cool with others when talking to them.

2.Express yourself in healthy ways

When you feel angry or upset with another person, it might be better to communicate this by talking with them about how they are making you feel rather than lashing out at them for their actions. This can help you overcome anger issues and prevent future situations from worsening.

3.Be patient with yourself

Remember that this problem needs to be resolved over time and will not be resolved in one day. Suppose you find that your anger issues are affecting your relationship negatively. In that case, you need to look closely at all of your relationships, as well as how they impact your professional life too. People from all walks of life can struggle with anger issues, and you need to examine all these areas to see if you might have a problem here. If you have anger issues, you're prone to being overreactive and angry at people. This can cause many problems in your personal and professional relationships, which is why you need to look closely at these areas if this is the case.

Chapter 3

COMMUNICATE YOUR WAY TO A HEALTHY RELATIONSHIP

C ommunication is more than just telling your partner what you want or think they should do. Communication isn't always a one-way street; it is also about listening to your partner and responding with actions that meet their needs. For your relationship to be successful, there needs to be effective communication between partners who are invested in building the relationship together, ensuring that both partners are on the same stage.

Effective communication that addresses the needs of both partners can enhance your connection and satisfaction over time, and helps you understand each other more deeply. For a successful relationship, it's crucial to possess the ability to actively listen and express your feelings effectively. It's essential to listen attentively and respond to your partner to ensure that both partners feel heard and comprehended. Provide your partner with the reassurance they need by clearly communicating your needs.

Effective communication is a critical component of any relationship. Although it may not be the most exciting subject to discuss, the more you and your partner communicate about your feelings, actively listen to each other, and communicate effectively, the stronger your relationship will become. When communicating with your partner, it's important to understand their perspective and role in the relationship. You can also learn about your partner's emotions and state of mind through nonverbal cues such as body language and tone of voice. This helps to identify if your partner is having an ordinary day or if they are upset, especially if they are similar in nature to you. Remember communication is a crucial aspect of relationships as it involves a two-way exchange, not just one. If the relationship starts to become lopsided, your partner may feel neglected or hurt by past actions or words.

COMMUNICATION BREAKDOWN: IDENTIFY AND FIX THEM NOW

Understanding the aspects of like-mindedness and differences between partners is an excellent basis for building your relationship. Learn to identify and respond to your partner's needs more efficiently. When you understand each other's needs and desires, tailor your communication strategies to accommodate that mindset change.

How is effective communication crucial for healthy relationships?

Effective communication is a key component in building and maintaining healthy relationships. Whether it be in a romantic relationship, friendship, or family dynamic, being able to effectively communicate helps to foster understanding, trust, and intimacy. One of the primary benefits of effective communication is increased understanding between you and your partner. When partners are able to openly and honestly communicate with one another, they can better understand each other's perspectives, feelings, and needs.

This will lead to a stronger bond and deeper emotional connection. By sharing thoughts and feelings, partners can build a deeper connection and understanding of one another. A couple who openly communicates about their individual wants and needs in a relationship is more likely to have a stronger, healthier relationship than a couple who keeps their thoughts and feelings to themselves. This in turn improves your intimacy and connection with your partner.

Another benefit of effective communication is increased trust. When you both can have open, honest conversations with each other, you are able to build trust and demonstrate your commitment to the relationship. A friend who confides in another about their personal struggles is more likely to build trust and deepen their friendship than a friend who keeps their struggles to themselves.

Also, when both partners can communicate effectively, it becomes easier to resolve conflicts that may arise in the relationship. For instance, you may be disagreeing about who should take care of household chores. By having an open and honest conversation, you can come to a solution that works for both. Good communication is a critical aspect of building trust in a relationship. When partners feel heard and understood, they are more likely to trust one another, even if there has been an experience of betrayal. The key to rebuilding trust is to have open and honest conversations where both partners can share their perspectives and understand each other's viewpoints.

Effective communication not only builds trust, but also provides emotional support in a relationship. When partners feel comfortable sharing their thoughts and feelings without fear of judgment, they feel more supported and less isolated. For instance, when one partner is going through a challenging time, they may need someone to talk to. By having a supportive and understanding conversation, the other partner can provide the emotional support they need to help them through their difficulties.

How can a lack of communication cause anger?

When partners are unable to effectively express their thoughts, feelings, and needs to each other it results in misunderstandings and unmet expectations, which can lead to feelings of frustration, disappointment, and anger. When partners don't communicate effectively, they may have different interpretations of events, leading to confusion and misinterpretation. This can create tension and cause anger, especially when one person feels that their thoughts and feelings are not being heard or respected.

A lack of communication can also lead to a breakdown in trust and intimacy, as partners may feel that they can no longer rely on each other to be open and honest. This can cause feelings of anger and betrayal and make it difficult for couples to resolve conflicts or work together towards common goals. To prevent a lack of communication from causing anger in a relationship, it is important for partners to actively listen to each other, express themselves clearly and respectfully, and try to understand each other's perspectives. It is also important to regularly check in with each other to make sure that everyone's needs, and expectations are being met, and to make an effort to work through any challenges that arise.

Common communication problems in relationships:

No one likes to feel ignored in a relationship because it feels as though you are not being heard. When people do not feel they are being listened to, they often become frustrated and shut down emotionally until they have their say. When partners cannot understand or listen to each other, it can lead to feeling like you do not care about their concerns or needs.

When communicating with your partner, you must take the time to listen and ensure that you understand them thoroughly before responding to make your response seem like you care about what your partner feels and wants from the relationship.

Here are some of the common communication problems:

1. Lack of Empathy

Emotions play a significant role in relationships. It is essential to listen to your partner when they share their concerns or thoughts with you. When you are unable to understand your partner, it can make them feel you do not care about their feelings or that you do not care about the relationship because of what is happening in their life. When people cannot express themselves effectively, it causes the individuals around them to feel as if they have no idea what their partner feels like or what their thoughts entail.

They will not understand why they are upset, leading to resentment and frustration within the relationship. The biggest problem in communication is not being able to feel or understand another person's point of view. When communicating, you must be empathetic towards one another and supportive.

Solution: Try to understand and accept your partner when they share their worries and concerns. If you cannot understand why they are upset, show them you care by asking them if you can help them. When communicating with your partner, try to listen attentively and clearly so you can better understand what they are saying.

2. Criticism

When you can communicate with your partner, it becomes easier to work towards solving problems together. When partners have difficulty communicating effectively, they often make critical statements about one another, which can lead to feeling criticized or ignored. This causes the relationship to fall apart because both parties cannot work through any problems and will not understand what is happening in the other person's life. Criticism can be a problem in relationships because some people are unable to understand how to give constructive criticism so that their partner knows how they can improve. When individuals learn from the criticisms they receive, they will be more effective in their everyday lives.

When people cannot receive criticism effectively, it can make them feel as though their life is out of control and that they will never be able to improve in the way they want because no one is willing or able to guide them.

Solution: When people cannot communicate effectively, they will assume that their partner is not trying to help them or show them a better way of life because they are critical of their actions. When this happens, it causes the person to feel that no one cares about what is going on in their life. When someone says something critical, try to find a way to work through the issue together as a couple. Work with them to determine the source of their frustration and encourage them to improve their abilities.

3. Defensiveness

When people feel defensive, it can lead to them being unable to work through their problems and effectively communicate with the people in their lives. When people cannot get through a difficult situation without getting defensive, it causes significant emotional distress. It often leads to resentment and anger that can result in hurt feelings. When individuals cannot express themselves clearly and effectively, they often take on a physical form of expression as they become angry or feel frustrated within the relationship.

People often don't understand why they are angry because they think they have no one who cares about them, which can cause stress in their relationships. When individuals feel defensive in their relationships, they must take the time to learn the skills they need to deal with their feelings and those around them effectively. Learning communication products will help you identify what you are feeling and communicate that effectively to understand better how to respond when your partner expresses it.

Solution: When you feel defensive, try to step back and take a deep breath to calm yourself. Think about how you can improve to understand what your partner is saying and why they are frustrated or upset. Take time to figure out how to better yourself to deal with the situations that arise in your relationships effectively. When you feel comfortable discussing problems openly with your partner, it will become easier for you to work through issues together and come up with solutions.

4. Blaming

When you cannot effectively communicate with your partner and understand what they are feeling, it can cause their feelings to get hurt or misunderstood. When you blame your partner or their behavior, it seems they have no control over their decisions, leading to resentment.

When individuals cannot express themselves effectively, it often causes them to lose control of their thoughts and feel that no one loves them anymore. People must learn how to deal with difficult situations without taking the blame for everything that happens within their relationship.

Solution: When you feel your partner is blaming you for their problems, try to communicate with them openly and honestly about what is going on. Getting through these issues makes it easier for you to come up with a solution together. Learn how to communicate effectively with your partner by acknowledging what they say and avoiding the blame game. Learning how to communicate with one another effectively can help you understand what happens in your relationship and will make it easier to deal with any problems that arise.

5. Passivity

Passivity is often a common problem in communication because people cannot express themselves boldly, which causes their relationships to begin to erode. Passive people often feel as though they have no voice in the relationship, so instead of speaking up, they end up staying quiet and feeling as though they do not affect their partner or the relationship that they are in.

Solution: When individuals become passive in their relationships, they tend to stop speaking up and letting their partner know how they feel. When this happens, it becomes more difficult for you to communicate effectively.

Take time to figure out what you are feeling and how you can express it to your partner so that you can work together to come up with a solution. When you effectively communicate, it will become easier for the two of you to understand each other.

Learning the skills, you need to interact and communicate with your partner effectively is important because it allows you to express yourself effectively. This can lead to a healthy relationship where both partners feel heard, understood, and loved.

Try out these communication skills by talking openly and honestly with your partner about the situation that has arisen. Take time to figure out your feelings so that you can devise a solution together.

LISTEN UP! THE ART OF ACTIVE LISTENING

Active listening is an excellent way to find out how well you're communicating with one another. Active listening to your partner will allow you to understand their concerns and thoughts so that you can solve problems correctly. When people cannot communicate with one another effectively, it can often cause them to lose interest or not see any point in continuing the relationship.

What is Active Listening?

When people feel as though they are not being appropriately listened to by their partner, it can often cause them to feel uncomfortable or insecure within the relationship because they do not feel heard. Active listening is a way to effectively communicate by listening to what your partner is saying without interrupting, challenging, or interfering with their speech. This method allows you to understand the inner feelings of your partner and be empathetic towards the situations they are facing. You will feel connected and understand how best to help each other when you feel frustrated, angry, or upset about something. Active listening is paying full attention to your partner, understanding their message, and providing an appropriate response.

Follow these steps to practice active listening with your partner:

1. Give your undivided attention to your partner and try to eliminate any distractions.

2. Show that you are listening, use nonverbal cues, such as nodding or making eye contact, to indicate that you are engaged in the conversation with them.

3. If you are not sure what your partner means, ask questions to clarify their message. This also sends them a signal that their message is being attentively received.

4. Reflect on what your partner is saying by paraphrasing their words and summarizing their message.

5. Try to understand your partners emotions and perspectives by putting yourself in their shoes.

6. Provide a thoughtful and appropriate response that shows that you have understood what your partner is conveying.

7. During the conversation always let them finish their thoughts and avoid interrupting them.

By following these steps, you are demonstrating that you are actively listening. When you listen actively, you will find that your partner feels safe and comfortable with you so that they can share their thoughts and feelings openly within the relationship and that you can understand one another better. Active listening can prevent conflicts within the relationship and help build trust and rapport with your partner.

Steps and strategies for practicing active listening in relationships:

Use the following strategies for practicing active listening when working with a partner:

1. Acknowledge what you hear

Communicating with your partner and understanding their feelings will strengthen the connection between the two of you. When people acknowledge what they have heard, they will be more willing to listen and understand each other's feelings. This will allow both partners to discuss the problem at hand and devise a practical solution that both partners feel comfortable with.

2. Reflection

Reflection is a powerful tool to use when you are trying to figure out the feelings of your partner and understand the situation that they are in. It allows you to talk about the emotions they are experiencing instead of focusing on the problem's reality to devise an effective solution. Reflection allows you to put yourself in their shoes and experience what they are feeling and give them a chance to solve problems productively.

3. Silence

Silence is often used as a tool because it allows people to feel comfortable speaking. When your partner feels nervous or unsure about what they should say, silence can help them be more confident in talking about their thoughts and views on situations.

4. Validate

When you can effectively understand your partner, you can empathize with their situation, making them more comfortable expressing their emotions. When people do not feel as though they can express themselves, they feel as though they are helpless in the situation, so when you can validate what they are experiencing, it shows them that there is someone who cares about them and wants to help alleviate their issues.

5. Seeking clarification or adding more detail

Understanding what your partner is feeling and experiencing will allow you to figure out how best to deal with the situation at hand, which will build trust between you and allow for a connection that strengthens your relationship.

6. Avoiding interrupting

Listening to someone without interrupting shows them they are being heard and will benefit from their thoughts and opinions. When you can avoid interrupting while listening, your partner will be more willing to talk with you because they feel they are being heard and understood.

7. Focus on the positive

When you can listen and understand what your partner is feeling and expressing, it shows that you care about their feelings and how happy they are within the relationship. This will allow them to see things from a more positive perspective because you want the best for them, which helps a stronger connection between you.

8. Repetition of the partner's words

When you both feel like you have to work together to find a solution that will benefit both parties, you can establish a more robust connection by repeating what each other has said. It demonstrates to your partner that you are there for them in a trying time and are trying to be of any assistance you can be when you can repeat what they have said.

9. Avoiding making assumptions

When you avoid making assumptions about how the situation will play out and what it will take for both partners involved in the relationship to feel safe, happy, and understood, it shows your partner that they can fully express themselves when there is no fear of judgment.

10. Summarize the issue

Summarizing the issue will allow both partners involved in the relationship to understand what is going on and how best to handle a specific situation. Outlining the issue will allow a stronger connection to form because you both feel you must work together for your relationships to be more successful.

SAY IT RIGHT!

Expressing anger in a healthy way

Anger is a normal and healthy emotion everyone deals with throughout life. Not everyone can express anger healthily, however. Expressing anger healthily allows both people to sympathize with one another's feelings. By feeling understood and accepted for your emotions, you will be able to find a solution together that will make you feel happier within the relationship. Expressing anger can help strengthen your relationships, but there are certain things that you must do if you want to be able to express anger healthily.

Healthy and unhealthy ways to express anger:

Constructive anger expression is when you can express your anger healthily and help find solutions together with your partner. Productive anger occurs when you can express your emotions in a manner your partner can understand and sympathize with. This will allow you to figure out how best to work together so that everyone feels happy within the relationship and has stronger connections between you.

Constructive expressions of anger will help strengthen your relationship because it shows that your partner cares about their feelings and want to be able to solve problems together. This happens because you both realize how important it is to work together and find a solution that benefits everyone involved in the relationship.

Passive-aggressive behavior is when you message that you do not care about your partner's feelings when angry with them. When you present yourself like this, it does not allow for a connection to form between the two of you because you are showing your partner that they are not wanted in the relationship and want to be left alone.

People who choose passive-aggressive behavior tend to avoid talking about their emotions and feelings. They will not feel as though they can express how they feel or how vulnerable they are, so they choose to be passive-aggressive with their feelings.

Being passive-aggressive shows your partner that you do not care about their feelings and want to avoid talking about them. This happens because your partner will leave you alone. After all, they cannot understand what you are doing or why you are doing it in a way that makes them feel uncomfortable. When partners choose this behavior, they avoid asking for help by using silent treatment, avoiding eye contact, turning off communication altogether, and other passive-aggressive tactics that will leave them feeling alone and isolated. Passive aggressive behavior can lead to people feeling as though they are not in a relationship because they do not feel the connection, they need to feel happy.

You can express anger healthily through:

1. Self-acceptance

It would be best if you accepted who you are and learned from your mistakes. Remember, everyone makes mistakes, and it is essential that you can find the opportunity to accept them so that you can look back on them in years to come. This will allow both parties involved in the relationship to move on and focus on what they want out of their relationships in the future.

2. Don't blame others

When people blame others for things they have done or emotions experienced, it is hard for them to fully understand what they have gone through and why they feel a certain way within the relationship. Once you know where they are coming from will allow you to empathize with them and help them feel as though they have been heard, which will lead to better communication within the relationship.

3. Avoid sarcasm

Sarcasm is expressing anger that allows you to talk down to someone and appear foolish when they emotionally express themselves. It would be best if you avoided sarcasm because it shows your partner that you do not care about what they have gone through or even how they feel, making them feel isolated in their relationship with you.

4. Avoid threats

Threats can seem like a way of expressing love, but in the long run, they can cause more harm than good. When you threaten your partner, you can make them feel like they cannot fully be themselves without being judged or ridiculed by you. This will make both partners unhappy because they cannot comfortably express themselves with their partner.

5. Avoid using names as an insult or criticism

Using names as insults or criticisms shows that you have very little respect for your partner and do not care how they feel within their relationship with you. You must avoid using names because it will allow you to sit back, understand what each of you has been through, find a solution together, and move on with the relationship feeling as though they have a better grasp on the situation. As we all know, expressing anger healthily can help strengthen our relationships. Suppose you do not express your anger healthily; in that case, it can adversely affect your relationship. Both of you will lose trust and begin to think negatively about one another, leaving both of you feeling lonely and insecure.

Here are ways through which anger is expressed unhealthily:

1. Being aggressive

Altering your moods to be aggressive and harmful to your partner can cause damage to your relationship. When you are angry, you do not need to be aggressive with your partner because they cannot understand what you are doing because they do not know how to behave in a manner that will help solve your problems.

2. Unwelcome words and actions

Using words meant for another person will cause them to feel unwanted in the relationship and could lead them away from the relationship. Words such as "You're fat," "You smell," or "You're ugly" are not acceptable ways to communicate with someone, but using such phrases can make people feel unwelcome in the relationship, which causes stronger connections between you and them.

3. Limiting your time with them

Choosing to limit the amount of time you spend with your partner when angry will force them to resent you because they feel they are being treated poorly and need to decide how best to get their needs met without your help. Additionally, choosing not to communicate about things that may be bothering you for a reason makes people feel as though they are being ignored and unwanted in the relationship.

4. Using threats

Threats can cause people to feel threatened because it shows that your partner does not have control over what happens between the two of you if they do not do what you want them to do for things to go the way they want them too. This can make them view you as a threat to the relationship because they feel like they cannot control their actions and have to put up with being treated poorly by you.

5. Judging and blaming

Blaming can show that you are not accepting of your partner or what they are saying. It can also cause the other person to feel embarrassed about the situation and may even offend them. Using this behavior will make your partner feel like they could not do anything to improve their situation because they have not done anything wrong. Being judgmental can make your partner feel as though they are not worth anything because you do not value them in the relationship.

6. Making comparisons

Comparisons can cause your partner to feel as though they are inferior. If you choose to make comparisons, it will make them feel inadequate or worthless in the relationship. Comparisons can also cause your partner to feel you do not value them and want to be left alone. Making comparisons can make your partner feel like they cannot measure up to who you want them to be or what you want from the relationship. Making such comparisons can lead to guilt, embarrassment, and anger because it shows that you are unhappy with how things are going and do not feel comfortable in the relationship.

7. Criticizing

Criticizing your partner can be hurtful to them because it shows that you do not value their opinion but instead choose to side with your own opinion. This could make them feel inferior because they do not matter in the relationship and must be left alone. If this happens, they may decide they do not want to be around you anymore and leave the relationship.

8. Ignoring their feelings

When your partner is angry and tells you how they feel or what bothers them, it can make them feel as though they are not wanted in the relationship because you choose not to speak of their feelings or show interest in what is going on with them. Ignoring them can make them feel as though they are not being heard, and it may also cause them to feel hurt or angry because you do not wish to speak with them. This could lead to your partner feeling invisible or unwanted in the relationship because they feel like they are losing a connection with you and that it would be better if they were alone.

These unhealthy expressions of anger can cause a strain on your relationship that is not needed. People should learn to express their anger healthily and productively. Learning how to express anger healthily will allow both partners involved in the relationship to sympathize with one another, leading to more beneficial, more trusting relationships between partners. Expressing anger healthily will lead to a more robust connection because when you show that you care and want to work together towards solutions, your partner feels more comfortable within the relationship.

CONFLICT RESOLUTION: THE PROVEN PATH TO HARMONIOUS RELATIONSHIP

Resolving conflicts instead of simply avoiding them will help you feel more confident in your relationship with your partner because they will begin to see its positive effect on their relationship.

How conflicts in relationships are inevitable and can lead to anger?

Conflicts cannot be avoided; they are an essential part of relationships. The two of you will have disagreements because people are different, which is typical in a relationship. These differences can lead to anger. Still, when these kinds of arguments arise, you must keep talking to one another to devise a solution so that you can move on with the relationship and focus on what you want out of your relationship in the future.

How can conflict lead to anger?

Couples who avoid conflict are likely to feel unsatisfied with their relationship because they will feel their partner is unwilling to work together towards a solution. It is essential that both of you can find a way to work together toward solutions. Despite the lack of trust or negative feelings, you can find a way towards being able to resolve the argument and move forward within your relationship because, in times of conflict, you must talk about what happened and how both of you can improve upon it so that it does not occur again within the future.

When we have conflicts, our heightened emotional states make them difficult for us to talk about calmly. We may have similar feelings when we are upset, resentful, or angry. Emotions intensify during conflicts so that our adversary is no longer a person but a demon who wishes to destroy everything we hold dear. We become blind to their situation and focus solely on our own. This is why it is essential to learn the art of expressing anger healthily, and this will allow the both of you to recognize that it happened, work together towards finding a solution together, and move forward within the relationship with positive feelings instead of negative ones and continue growing your relationship in the future.

Unresolved conflict can lead to anger because people tend to feel as though they are left alone for prolonged periods, which leads them to feel as though they have no one around to talk to and express their emotions. When you feel like you have no one around you, it is your responsibility to make sure that you can healthily express your feelings so that both of you can move on with the relationship and past the issue causing conflict within the relationship. "In certain relationships, anger can become a major issue because it can cause your partner to feel as though you feel as though their feelings are invalid or even wrong.".

Clarifying your needs and wants within a relationship is very important because it will allow you to express what you need and want instead of feeling as though you have no idea when they are expected to meet these expectations. Unresolved conflict is a big problem that most couples face because it creates an environment that can cause both partners to feel angry, resentful, and even frustrated whenever they do not get what they want out of their relationship.

Steps and strategies for healthily resolving conflicts:

The best way to resolve a dispute healthily is by understanding where the problem comes from and recognizing your actions' impact on your partner. This is important within a relationship because it lets you know how to change your behaviors and think about resolving conflicts with your partner more positively.

1. Confronting an issue

Confronting an issue or problem is obvious but prudent when it comes to resolving conflict in a healthy way which will allow for both of you to work together towards coming up with a solution together because it shows that both of you want the same thing out of this relationship and are willing to take steps towards making this possible for each other.

2. Compromise

Compromise is an essential part of this discussion because it allows you to understand that you and your partner want the same thing out of this relationship which is for it to be healthy. If you are willing to compromise with one another, you will be able to create a healthy bond between you and understand what your partner wants out of this relationship so that moving forward within the relationship; there will not be any issues in the future.

3. Collaboration

Partners will become frustrated with one another when they argue, and they tend to get resentful towards their partner. When this happens, you must take some time out of your day to talk about what happened and why it happened so that you can evaluate your relationship. It is also essential to understand the root of the conflict so that moving forward within the relationship, there are no more issues because you have already evaluated the problem within your relationship and are working together towards finding a solution.

4. Empathy

Empathy is essential to resolving conflicts within your relationship because it allows you to share emotions with your partner and feel what they are going through. By being empathetic, you can recognize your actions' impact on one another. This allows you to work together towards a solution that will prevent issues from happening again.

5. Evaluating oneself

Another critical aspect of conflict resolution is evaluating an individual's past behavior within the relationship so that they can recognize their shortcomings and improve upon these situations in the future so that avoiding conflicts is easy when moving forward with their partner in the future.

6. Building emotional intelligence

When partners can communicate with one another, they will be able to keep their emotions in check. This will allow for a healthier environment within the relationship because you have evaluated the conflict and come up with a solution as a couple which is excellent. After all, it allows both partners to have happy feelings instead of unpleasant ones.

7. Seeking healthy advice

This is another crucial step because it allows both partners to seek advice from people they trust within the relationship, and this can even be outside of the relationship, such as a family member, friend, or counsellor, and this will ensure that you come up with an effective solution together.

When you resolve conflicts within your relationship, it will help both of you be able to express your needs and wants instead of feeling as though you are unable to express them within the relationship because it will allow both of you to understand what is going on, how each party feels within the relationship and move on from there together. Resolving conflicts will enable both partners in the argument to feel they are moving forward with their relationship and no longer overwhelmingly angry with one another.

Chapter 4

COPING STRATEGIES FOR ANGER MANAGEMENT

A nger is the fuel that fuels most heated arguments. It can be challenging to understand, analyze and manage your anger to move through conflict constructively. Coping strategies are tools you can use to de-escalate conflict and promote healing within your relationship and outside of it.

TAKE A TIME-OUT: POWERFUL TECHNIQUE TO CALM YOURSELF DOWN

Time-out involves physically removing yourself from the situation or person, making you angry. Time-out can be defined as leaving the room to gather your thoughts and get yourself together, or it can refer to taking time away from your partner for a specific period, such as 30 minutes, to cool off.

Time-outs are especially useful when dealing with anger over things done or said repeatedly. Time-out is an excellent way to realize that this situation has gotten out of hand before it leads to an argument. It also allows you time to think about how you will respond when the other person apologizes and realizes what they have done wrong.

These time-out techniques include:

1. Walking away from the situation or person until you can calm down enough to think again. This will also allow the other person time to calm down, preventing any acting out by either one of you in anger.

2. Take a cool shower or bath to calm yourself down. The cool water can relax tense muscles and help clear your head. Some people find that it also helps them fall asleep at night if they are feeling anxious or stressed and need to get their minds off their problems and relax.

3. Take a drive in the car and listen to some music, especially some soothing music, so you can relax and clear your mind.

4. Meditate: Sit quietly with your eyes closed and concentrate on your breathing, counting each breath as it comes in and goes out. This will help clear your mind of anger, so you can think more clearly again about how to handle the situation at hand once you've calmed down enough to be rational again.

5. Talk to a friend about the situation or person who got you upset. This will allow you to express your anger and frustration over how things have gone and the intensity of their hurtful behavior towards you.

6. Write in your journal about how you feel, how angry you are, what needs to be done, and why it is crucial. Then place it beside your bed so that you can see it every night before bedtime

7. Write a letter to the person or situation that upset you. Write down exactly what happened or what they said that made you so angry and how it made you feel about them (i.e., embarrassing, hurt, frustrated). Then take a few days before giving it to them to read so that it won't be fresh in your mind anymore, and you can deal with the situation more rationally.

Use these time-out techniques to understand your perspectives, needs, and feelings, and you must learn how to separate yourself from these feelings by observing them and not acting upon them.

Benefits of taking a time-out during an argument:

Taking a time-out during an argument will help you to regain control of your feelings, especially if you are prone to violent outbursts. Time-outs help devise a plan of action and allow time to calm down and reflect. You can use this time to think about your anger and how it can be channeled more positively rather than focusing on the negative aspects of the conflict or the negative words or actions directed towards you.

It will help you develop a plan of action and think about what steps you will take to reach an understanding with your partner.

It will help you restore self-regard by keeping you cool, taking an objective look at the situation, and realizing that there are always better ways to deal with conflict than lashing out. Suppose you learn how to respond to disputes healthily rather than resorting to aggressive behaviors. In that case, you will be placing yourself in a better position for success and resolution. It is about temporarily removing yourself from a toxic environment, whether it be behavior or physical space that has become toxic.

Helps you maintain your mental toughness. This is a crucial advantage because it is much simpler for someone to bring up the subject again and make it worse when you are upset and acting negatively. By preventing this from happening and giving you some time to collect yourself, taking a break can help you avoid conflict from escalating and harming your relationship.

It is also essential that you figure out how you will react when the other person apologizes, how you will address issues that may have come up during the argument, and ways that the two of you can work together to move past this temporary setback. This will help you become more aware of how each of your actions impacts the other, which can lead to more positive interactions and relationships.

Steps and strategies for taking a time-out:

Taking a time-out from an argument can be done a few different ways, such as leaving the room and taking a walk or going somewhere the two of you can have privacy. These steps allow you to regain control of your emotions and create space between yourselves to start understanding how the conflict makes you feel.

Strategies for taking a time-out include:

• Physically removing yourself from the situation

Physically removing yourself from the situation prevents the potential for physical violence and allows both of you to cool off. This helps prevent damage to your relationships, as well as your ego. If you are angry with someone, it is understandable that you would have a desire or impulse to lash out physically; however, this is counterproductive and can lead to negative results. Taking a time-out allows you to reflect on what makes you angry, so you can deal with it more constructively the next time it comes up.

• Finding a calming activity

Taking a walk or finding another relaxing activity that helps you calm down could positively affect your anger management. It can be very beneficial to listen to music, meditate, exercise, or even read a book. These activities will help you calm your mind and help you think more clearly; that way, when the time is right for you two to resolve the issue, you will be able to do so in a constructive manner.

• Setting a time limit for the time-out

Setting a time limit for the time-out lets you know when you will have cooled down and when it will be safe for you to interact with your partner again. This can help prevent confusion or suspicion and prevent you from engaging in a heated argument that could lead to negative consequences. You may also want to set a time limit for yourself, such as an hour or two after the fact.

• Recounting what happened verbally and non-verbally

Once you have cooled off, recount what happened verbally and non-verbally. Non-verbal conflict can be just as damaging as verbal conflict, so you must be able to communicate how you feel constructively. This can help avoid misunderstandings and hurt feelings and help you come to a constructive resolution.

• Discuss how you each feel about the situation

Once you have verbally recounted what happened and reflected upon it, you can discuss how both of you feel about the situation, which can help understand one another's feelings and reactions. Once again, this is an essential step to prevent future arguments from becoming too heated or destructive.

Taking a time-out from an argument gives both partners a chance to separate from each other and allow their feelings and emotions about what has happened during the argument to dissipate. By not responding in a heated manner, you can give both of you a chance to cool off and reflect on how the discussion has gone. It also allows everyone involved to take more time to think about what happened and how they might make things better.

If taking a time-out during an argument does not work for you or your partner, then it may be possible for you two to agree upon other strategies to resolve conflict more effectively than arguing over hurtful words. This can be done by talking about what happened; it may not resolve everything, but it will allow you to know where you stand as far as your relationship is concerned and help each of you deal with things less destructively.

If there is a lot of arguing, you must agree on handling the situation. One person may feel that they are the victim, and they want them to punish or "pay" for their actions. It may be possible for one partner to stay quiet when this happens if the other partner stays calm and talks about how they are feeling.

RELAX AND RECHARGE: PROVEN TECHNIQUES TO ACHIEVE PEACEFUL SERENITY

Relaxation techniques are a popular form of mental, emotional, and physical exercise. These techniques may help with anger management and prevent or reduce the frequency or intensity of what has made you angry. When used in conjunction with other skills in anger management, they can be beneficial in helping you handle conflicts and better communication.

The most effective relaxation technique will depend on your personal needs and preferences regarding stress. Some people prefer to use guided imagery with music, bodywork, touch therapy, and imagery; others might prefer to use information about the emotions of others' experiences through reading or watching videos on emotional regulation. Relaxation techniques can be beneficial in allowing you to think clearly and rationally while trying to resolve an argument. In a relationship, if both partners are willing to understand one another's emotions, a second reading might be needed during a time-out when people are calmer and more relaxed.

You can use relaxation techniques while discussing the issue that has caused you anger. The time-out can help cool things down and allow the two of you to discuss how you feel without being too emotionally involved in the situation. Relaxation techniques may also prevent future arguments or let the two of you have calm discussions without resorting to anger to resolve conflict.

The physical and psychological benefits of relaxation:

The physical and psychological benefits of relaxation can help prevent you from becoming too emotionally involved in an argument. In turn, this can help you manage anger more constructively and allow your partner to understand your feelings without resorting to threatening or fighting words. Helping you relax and regroup after an argument may make it easier to discuss how you feel rationally without becoming too emotional.

The physical benefits of relaxation in a relationship include:

1. Reducing muscle tension: Muscle tension occurs when you have been physically or emotionally stressed. Relaxation techniques can help reduce this muscle tension and make you feel calmer and more relaxed. For example, if you and your partner have been arguing, you might feel anxiety and muscle tension. Helping to relax those muscles can help prevent further injury or harm when communicating with your partner.

2. Improving sleep disorders: Many people with difficulty sleeping due to stress may benefit from relaxation techniques as part of their treatment plan. Relaxation techniques can be done while lying in bed, which can help you fall asleep more efficiently and reduce the probability that you will wake up during the night due to an argument or a stressful dream. If you use relaxation techniques effectively, it may be easier for both of you to fall asleep and stay asleep throughout the night.

3. Lowering your blood pressure: High blood pressure can increase your risk of heart disease, heart attack, and stroke, all severe life-threatening conditions that can occur when you are stressed out. Relaxation techniques can lower your blood pressure, making it easier for you to handle stress and anger healthily. For example, you might raise your blood pressure if your partner is angry during an argument. This is a natural response to stressful situations, which can cause harm to your circulatory system. Using relaxation techniques during an argument can help lower your blood pressure and prevent further damage to your circulatory system.

4. Reducing muscle aches and pains: Muscles can become sore (and even injured) if you become too tense or stressed out for an extended period. Relaxation techniques can reduce muscle tension and help prevent pain or injury when you are in a relationship with someone angry or upset over something that happened during the day at work or school. By using relaxation techniques, you can benefit from the physical therapy that results from your efforts.

The physical benefits of relaxation can help you handle stress and anger more constructively and healthily. By reducing your risk of heart disease, stroke, and heart attack, relaxation techniques can help you live longer and happier. Relationships can be complicated but improving your ability to relax can help you resolve issues and reduce stress. Helping your partner relax can benefit both of you physically and emotionally.

It is also possible for relaxation techniques to help lower blood pressure and muscle tension when participating in an argument, which can prevent further physical harm or injury as a result of expressing anger.

Although relaxation techniques are not considered a treatment for anger management, they can positively affect your overall emotional and physical health. Relaxation techniques can help improve your sleep quality, blood pressure level, muscle health, and overall sense of well-being; all of which can lead to fewer arguments in the home.

The psychological benefits of relaxation. The psychological benefits of relaxation in a relationship can be very beneficial when used correctly. Relaxation techniques allow you to discuss the issue at hand rationally and calmly. You might feel like yelling or screaming at one another because of stress or anger. Still, by using these techniques, it may be possible for you to feel more comfortable discussing the issue without having to resort to threatening or using physical force during an argument. Remember that once your partner feels understood, they may be more willing to discuss how they feel with you rather than resort to physical violence during an argument.

The psychological benefits of relaxation include:

1. Reducing stress: Stress occurs when you feel like you cannot cope with the demands of your life. Feeling stressed may make it difficult for you to reason, which can cause problems within your relationship. You might feel like arguing or fighting with your partner because you do not want to deal with the issue calmly. Relaxation techniques can reduce stress, making it easier to discuss how you feel and how the issue at hand can be resolved.

2. Improving your ability to handle anger: Anger is often considered a natural part of life and a healthy emotion that can be used constructively if managed effectively. By using relaxation techniques, you can constructively express your anger without resorting to physical violence or being verbally abusive. Relaxation techniques can help

you communicate how you feel calmly and rationally, making it easier for your partner to understand how they can better handle the issue.

3. Increasing personal confidence: Many people who become angry or stressed out believe that they are unable to cope with their problems and turn to alcohol, drugs, or promiscuous sex as an escape from their problems. By using relaxation techniques, you can increase your confidence and feel better about yourself when handling stress and anger healthily. The more confidence you have in managing stress and anger, the more likely you will make positive decisions regarding your relationship with your partner.

4. A sense of control: Relaxation techniques can help provide a sense of control, which many people feel they lack in their lives, at least temporarily in some cases. Feeling like you have control in your relationship can reduce the risk of arguments. If you do not feel like you have any control over your relationship, you will probably feel more like an object than an equal partner. Maintaining power over your actions and decisions can help reduce stress in a relationship, resulting from feeling out of control over what happens.

5. Improved memory: Many studies show that relaxation techniques such as meditation and yoga improve memory. When you can relax, it allows your mind to feel refreshed and alert when discussing an issue with your partner. By using relaxation techniques, the ability to recall important information will be easier for both of you, which can constructively resolve the issue.

6. Increased creativity: Relaxation techniques can increase your ability to think creatively, which will help you resolve the issue at hand creatively. When you can think creatively, it may be easier for both of you to resolve the issue creatively that does not involve physical violence or verbal abuse.

7. Self-realization: Relaxation helps us see ourselves for who we truly are, a person who deserves respect and love from others. While acting out of anger and frustration during an argument may be tempting, relaxing your muscles allows you to see yourself for who you are. Being self-aware is a skill many people lack, so feeling like we have control over

our actions can empower us. Relaxing our muscles allows us to become more aware of our emotions and how we choose to act in our lives.

The psychological benefits of relaxation can help make it easier for both of you to communicate how you feel and resolve the issue at hand using constructive conflict-resolution strategies. If you can discuss how you feel using rational and calm communication, your partner can understand how they can improve their behavior without resorting to physical violence or verbal abuse during an argument.

TECHNIQUES FOR RELAXATION:

When it comes to feeling calm and relaxed, especially one that improves your ability to handle anger and stress, you must select the right techniques for you and your partner. If you are uncomfortable with any of these techniques, you can try a different technique to see if it works better for your relationship.

1. Yoga: This is one of the most popular relaxation techniques, and many couples do yoga together to improve their relationship. If you think that yoga may be helpful for you and your partner, then you can take some time each day to practice yoga together. The main advantage of yoga is that it helps improve your body and mind as you relax during a session. Yoga can help you learn how to relax through your body, making it easier to calm down when working out a problem with your partner. When you can calm down and relax healthily, resolving issues becomes more manageable for you.

2. Meditation: Many people use meditation as a stress reduction tool because it allows them to focus on the present moment. When we meditate, we use our minds to achieve a relaxed state. When we can focus on the present moment, we can feel comfortable and reduce our anxiety about the problem. Meditating can help us focus on how we think without focusing on issues that cause us stress. Meditation can be done by yourself or with your partner. When you want to meditate together, it helps if both of you find a comfortable place to sit back-to-back and focus on being in the present moment together. While you don't need to use the same technique as your partner, it does help if both of you use compatible techniques. For example, it can help if you both use the same technique when meditating together.

3. Breathing exercises: One of the oldest methods for relaxation is breathing exercises, which can help reduce stress, slow down your heart rate, and improve overall health. It only takes a few minutes each day to practice breathing exercises with your partner, but the results can last all day long. Each partner needs to practice different breathing techniques, which each of you can do during an argument. You may use many breathing techniques, and each works better for some people than others. For example, one person may be more likely to feel more relaxed when they focus on deep breathing, while their partner is more likely to feel calmer when they focus on the rhythm of their breathing. It would be best to find a technique that works for you so you can relax after an argument without resorting to abuse.

4. Progressive muscle relaxation: A Progressive muscle relaxation is a form of deep breathing that has the benefit of helping you to relax your muscles as you are breathing. This technique helps to release muscle tension in the body, which can be very helpful for those who get muscle spasms, aches, and pains regularly. Progressive muscle relaxation helps you recognize where the tension is in your body and enables you to release them. When we learn to relax our muscles, it becomes easier to manage our anger because it helps us understand how our body responds during an argument. For example, suppose we can identify that our breathing becomes rapid when we get angry. In that case, we can practice deep breathing and release tension in the body without resorting to fighting with our partner.

When practicing progressive muscle relaxation, follow these steps:

1. Choose a place to sit comfortably and concentrate on what your body feels like.

2. When you are ready to begin, close your eyes and focus on breathing. Make sure that you can breathe deeply with each breath. Try to breathe from the diaphragm and allow each breath to fill your lungs

3. When you have completed a couple of breaths, move your attention to your feet. Focus on how they feel at this moment in time. If you notice something that hurts or is uncomfortable, spend a few moments relaxing before moving

on.

4. You must keep breathing deeply as you pay attention to each part of the body until you reach the top of the head.

5. When you have completed the entire body, you must go back to your feet again and notice how they feel this time. You may want to make a few changes so that they feel relaxed again.

Suppose you are using progressive muscle relaxation with your partner. In that case, you can repeat this process together to help each other relax after an argument. By practicing progressive muscle relaxation with your partner, you can learn how to physically release tension when you are feeling angry or tense during an argument.

5. Visualization: Visualization is one of the more creative ways to reduce stress and tension. When we visualize, we create an image that helps us achieve a different reality than we are experiencing. When you use visualization, you should be able to picture yourself in a safe place where you will not be hurt by anyone or anything and feel like you can relax entirely at any time. You can use this technique for relaxation or positive self-talk. It is easy to use visualization as part of your self-talk if your partner constantly criticizes and belittles your thoughts and feelings. Being able to visualize yourself in a carefree place, can help you to recover from the emotional trauma of your partner's constant criticism.

Visualization techniques can be done together as partners, and it is beneficial for you to use methods that are suitable for your partner. If you use the same technique but your partner is uncomfortable, you may want to switch to a different one. It can also help if you spend some time practicing each technique separately so that each of you is familiar with it when practicing together. You can also use visualization exercises in verbal self-talk and when communicating with your partner and have one of you act out the visualization. In contrast, the other person acts out verbal self-talk. Using visualization techniques with your partner makes it possible to heal from your past trauma and help them heal from their past hurts.

When you know how to relax your body, then you may be able to manage your anger without resorting to yelling and arguing. When you can identify the physical signs that you are stressed or uncomfortable, then it will help you release tension without hurting your partner. Both of you need to learn various relaxation techniques and find which works best for you before arguing to prevent verbal abuse from occurring during an argument. In addition, relaxation exercises can also help partners understand how their bodies respond during stressful moments. If you become angry enough that you need to hurt your partner, it can help you slow down and relax your body before acting on your anger. If you combine relaxation techniques with verbal self-talk, you can release tension while minimizing your level of anger.

THE POWER OF MINDFULNESS: A TOOL TO HEAL AND TRANSFORM

Mindfulness is an important skill to have if you want to learn how to manage your anger. Mindfulness helps you become aware of your thoughts and emotions without judging them as right or wrong. Mindfulness allows you to notice what is going on around you without falling into the trap of questioning everything that your partner says.

Mindfulness helps you to have a different attitude when talking with your partner. It allows you to recognize that they are hurting and begin by making positive suggestions before suggesting negative comments that may make your partner feel bad about themselves or their behavior. Learning to be mindful of one another may help both of you to find the peacefulness and carefree nature of the relationship again.

What is Mindfulness?

Mindfulness can be defined as an attitude where you can be aware of what is happening around you without being judgmental. It is important to note that mindfulness does not mean you do not have standards. Instead, it means that when your partner behaves unacceptably, instead of judging them, you will be able to calmly tell them why their behavior was wrong without becoming angry or defensive. When you can speak with your partner and respond calmly, it will help them to change their behavior over time so that they can be the kind of person you want them to be for a long-lasting relationship. Mindfulness is essential in helping you to control your anger when speaking with your partner. When you can be mindful, then it will help you avoid becoming angry or saying hurtful things that could destroy your relationship. Although many people think that mindfulness means you do not have standards and will allow anyone to behave however, they want, this is not true. Instead, a person who is being mindful will calmly reason with their partner and tell them why their behavior is wrong without becoming angry or defensive about it.

If you become upset with your partner for their behavior, it can cause further fighting between you because one of you could get defensive and make the other feel bad about what they did or said. This can cause both of you to want to hurt the other person. However, this is less likely to happen if you can be mindful with one another. Instead, you will be able to understand why your partner is doing something and suggest ways that they could change their behavior. If you explain to your partner that their behavior made you angry or upset, it will help them get in touch with what they are feeling and become aware that their behavior may hurt or make you angry.

How can mindfulness be used as a coping strategy for managing anger?

Mindfulness also allows you to recognize your partner's feelings without becoming angry or defensive. It can help you to be aware of what your partner may be thinking or feeling so that you do not communicate with them in a way that will cause them to feel embarrassed or ashamed of themselves. You want to make sure that you can see the world through your partner's eyes, so it helps if you notice how they are reacting to situations and respond in a way that includes them. If you become frustrated with your partner for something they did or said, then both of you can have an argument where neither of you gives into the temptation of getting angry and attacking one other with hurtful words. Instead, you will be able to calmly explain why their behavior was wrong without blaming them or making them feel like they are not good enough for you.

Mindfulness can help you recognize the moment you are getting upset and stay calm while discussing with your partner. Instead of telling them why their behavior was not correct, it is possible for your discussion to become heated and filled with hurtful comments that can destroy your relationship. Learning to be mindful may also help you realize that they are not bad and could change over time if they want to. Mindfulness is essential in helping you to manage your anger when speaking with your partner. When you can be mindful, then it will help you avoid becoming angry or saying hurtful things that could destroy your relationship. Although many people think that mindfulness means you do not have standards and will allow anyone to behave however, they want, this is not true.

Instead, a person who is being mindful will calmly reason with their partner and tell them why their behavior is wrong without becoming angry or defensive about it. If you become upset with your partner for their behavior, it can cause further fighting between you because one of you could get defensive and make the other feel bad about what they did or said. This can cause both of you to want to hurt the other person.

Tips for incorporating mindfulness into daily life and in managing anger in relationships:

1. Paying attention to the present moment: Instead of thinking about something that happened in the past, it is essential always to be aware of the present moment. When you can pay attention to the present moment, it gives you a sense of control over what is happening around you so that you will not become angry or upset. When your partner becomes upset at something, they may try to take their anger out on other people, which could cause you to get upset without even realizing it. For example, when your partner is not mindful, they may get upset when people cut them off in traffic and retaliate by driving recklessly. Sometimes, it could cause your partner to yell at someone for something that is not their fault. However, if you can recognize the present moment and notice your feelings, you will stay calm and realize it is not worth getting angry or trying to hurt someone because of your partner's actions.

2. Acknowledging and accepting emotions without judgment: When you can remember that your partner is a human being, you will be able to recognize that they may have

good and bad days. In other words, they may be angry when it is inappropriate to their behavior or when they are upset with you. However, if this causes them to become angry and try to hurt others, then it is up to both of you what kind of relationship you are willing to maintain. If one of you is being obtuse or dismissive with their anger, it can cause both people in the relationship to become defensive and upset.

3. Letting go of painful thoughts that cannot be changed: If you can let go of specific thoughts, it will help alleviate the pain that comes from holding on to those feelings. For example, if your partner does something you find offensive, it can make you angry and hurt. If you want to avoid acting on this anger, you should realize that it was unintentional and may have been caused by a lack of mindfulness. For example, if your partner is being forgetful or does not clean up after themselves when they cook for the family when all of your children are with them, then it can cause both of you to be angry because neither one wants to be kept waiting or have food left over. This can make you feel angry, upset, and hurt because of their behavior, and in some cases, it could cause a fight between you. However, if you can acknowledge that it was not intentional and that your partner may not have been aware of their actions, it will be less likely for your feelings to be hurt and for the two of you to get into an argument. If one of you is mindful, they will be able to recognize when they are critical or judgmental because they do not see things through your partner's eyes. However, if you are not mindful, then it can cause both of you to get angry or upset with one another without realizing why.

4. Being kind and compassionate towards yourself: If you can see that you tend to get angry when your partner is inconsiderate of your feelings, it can help you acknowledge that it is a side effect of being unconscious. For example, you can argue about how angry each other feels when both of you are upset, and neither one can think of what has angered them the most. However, if you were paying close attention, you would realize that this argument could have been avoided if one or both of you had been mindful and acknowledged the feelings that the other was having.

5. Being generous with your partner: When you can appreciate your partner for what they do, it can help make both of you feel closer to one another. In the same way, if

you openly communicate about the things that bother you with one another, then it can help eliminate some of the things that will upset or anger you in the first place. One member of a couple can be overly critical and judgmental of their spouse without realizing what they are doing. In some cases, they may get angry at their spouse because they are hurt and upset but unable to express their feelings. When this happens, both partners need to be mindful to be open with one another and help each other overcome the challenges in their relationship.

Being mindful will allow you to recognize your feelings and determine the difference between what anger is and what is realistic in a relationship. In addition, it helps those who can become more conscious of their emotions because they will not get upset as quickly when they see something their partner does that bothers them. Being mindful of your feelings, situation, and actions will help with keeping the relationship together because there will be less arguing about things that are not worth getting angry about if for no other reason than you decide not to fight in the first place.

REFRAME YOUR THOUGHTS: HOW TO TURN NEGATIVITY INTO POSITIVITY

To help with your relationship, you must reframe your negative thoughts. You may be angry at your partner when they forget to pick up their child from daycare and leave a pile of clothes in the middle of the bedroom floor. However, if they are being forgetful, this may be without meaning to hurt you or others. It is important to remember that your partner may not even realize that they are being hurtful. If they do not learn that this makes you upset and angry, then there is no point in getting upset with them because it will only cause you to fight about something that may not matter in any way. If they do not know that this is upsetting you, it will likely only make you more upset with them because they are upsetting you in the first place.

Sometimes, this can cause one partner to get angry with the other because they do not understand why the other person is upset. The problem may be that it is hard for you to communicate how you feel about certain things. For example, if one partner takes a long time to pick up their child from daycare or forgets to put food on the table when everyone else has eaten and leaves a mess, both of you may be irritated or think that your partner is inconsiderate and forgetful.

However, if this was not intended to be hurtful to you and your partner, it may not be worth getting angry about if you are mindful. This will help to eliminate arguments that can cause misunderstandings, hurt feelings, hurt bodies, and create a negative atmosphere.

All relationships have differences between the two of you. If someone is angry or upset because they cannot find something they need to complete at work or in their free time, it can be frustrating because they need it badly. They may feel that their partner has been inconsiderable and unmindful when they try to complete what is crucial for them.

How can negative thoughts contribute to anger?

A person may be angry because they think their partner is inconsiderable and un-mindful of what they are doing, or they may be angry because they feel they have to do everything in the relationship. This can cause someone to become hurt, upset, and angry if they cannot communicate these feelings to their partner.

These feelings can cause the person who is upset to feel and act inappropriately. The other partner will react by arguing with them or retaliating against them for being hurtful and unpleasant in ways that only fuel the fire. This will lead to a downward spiral in which you get more irritated, aggravated, upset, and angry with one another without realizing how your thoughts are causing you distress.

Negative thoughts can contribute to anger because people tend to think in a way that worsens their rage. Negative reviews are more likely than positive ones, and this is because negative thinking leads to a lot of frustration. This type of thinking is also referred to as cognitive distortion. For example, if you are upset that your partner left their dirty clothes in the middle of the bedroom floor and you're thinking about how inconsiderate they are, this can cause you to get angry with them.

This thinking is negative because it only focuses on what your partner has done wrong. It is unfair to them because it does not allow for any alternative explanation that may be more reminiscent of the situation. In addition, if you think negatively enough about the situation, then it may cause you to become overwhelmed by anger and hurt feelings.

In cognitive distortions, people tend to overgeneralize certain events and make assumptions about something that can never be tested for. For example, if you overgeneralize about your partner leaving their dirty clothes on the bedroom floor and get mad at them for it, then you are assuming that they are being inconsiderable. It is unlikely that this will happen again any time soon because they were not being inconsiderate the first time.

It is more likely that they had forgotten to put away dirty clothes in the first place or had not had a chance to wash them up before they left their house. When someone thinks negatively enough about the situation, these thoughts can lead to irrational behavior and cause an explosion of rage in one person or a scapegoat effect in which one person feels like they are always blaming another person for everything wrong in their relationship with them.

The role of cognitive distortions in anger

Cognitive distortions are thinking errors and significantly impact how people feel about the world around them. Some of these distortions can make it hard to determine what is true or false depending on how you think about a situation. They can cause you to think negatively enough to do something irrational because the anger that they cause is unreasonable.

When someone has negative thoughts that lead them to anger, they may feel like their partner is always doing something wrong or that they don't exist in their relationship. If this happens often enough, then this will make them even angrier with one another without realizing why this is happening in the first place.

People experiencing intense anger often use cognitive distortions to think about a situation. In some cases, they may have difficulty telling the difference between what is happening around them and how they perceive it. Sometimes these distorted ways of thinking can make it hard for someone to respond appropriately if someone does something inconsiderate or unmindful of what another person needs from them.

An example would be if your partner forgot to turn off the refrigerator when leaving their house, and you got angry. Then you might have negative thoughts about your partner failing to turn off the refrigerator, even though that was not true. In addition, these thoughts can cause you to act irrationally and make you feel like your partner being inconsiderable was a cause of your anger.

Negative thoughts are not always something that causes anger. Some types of anger can lead to these negative thoughts in one way or another, which can harm the relationship and lead to more problems for the angry person than had the situation been handled rationally.

Steps and strategies for reframing negative thoughts:

Reframing negative thoughts can be done daily to help deal with anger. This can help to control how a person feels and allows one to make better decisions because they are more aware of their emotions and thoughts. Here are some steps and strategies that can be used to reframe negative thoughts:

1. Acknowledge that your negative thoughts are occurring: So many people try to avoid these thoughts or ignore them because they do not want to face what their anger is about. This can cause problems in the relationship because it does not allow the partners to work on their issues together and see what needs to be addressed more effectively. This is another reason why it is essential for people experiencing anger in a relationship (or who have experienced anger within the relationship) to reframe these thoughts and know that they are not always true.

2. Consider the other side of the story: Sometimes people jump to conclusions when they feel like they are being personally attacked. Other times, they think about how their partner's behavior affects them instead of how their partner feels about what is happening around them. These behaviors can make it hard for a person to work through their anger effectively if they do not consider what the situation might be like

from their partner's perspective and what role their thoughts and emotions have played in their responses.

3. Be fair in your thinking about what is happening: A person needs to examine the facts of an issue happening to them to make sense of it and clear up any misconceptions they might have. Sometimes, people might have difficulty understanding why their partner is acting the way they are because they only see what is happening from their perspective. If a person can look at the whole situation from a realistic point of view, they can often gain a better understanding of what is going on.

4. Consider other options for responding to your partner's behavior when it occurs: Sometimes people take actions that will make the situation worse and do not think about how they could have been more effective in resolving the issue they are upset with. It might be possible to work out an issue without having to react in an aggressive or hostile manner and without feeling hurt by your partner's behavior. It is essential to consider how the person you are angry with might have responded to your behavior and how they might have created a better outcome for both of you.

5. Experiment with ways to respond differently instead of acting on your negative thoughts: People can often be stressed out about situations between them and their partners, causing them to react in ways that will make things worse than if they had handled those situations more calmly. It is essential for people experiencing anger in relationships to experiment with different responses so that they can see what works best for them and what does not work according to their partner's response.

6. Evaluate your relationship and think about how you can communicate with your partner better in the future: People need to examine their communication styles with their partners so that they know how to be more effective in the future. Sometimes what they are doing is not working because it is not getting them through to the other person. It can also cause many problems if a person takes things personally because it will lead to quarrels and arguments within the relationship that could have otherwise been avoided. Learning skills for effective communication can help a person greatly in their relationships and also help them relieve some of the stress caused by problems that occurred in the past.

There are many ways that people experiencing anger in a relationship can deal with this feeling. The best method of dealing with it is often to have patience and be willing to work through the issue, taking time to address the real issues causing the anger. A person can try discussing with their partner and see what they can do together, or they can try having a conversation alone so that they are both in charge of the situation.

It is also essential for a person to try to look at the situation from their partner's perspective and understand why they may be acting in a certain way. This can help both people feel better about the situation to overcome the real issue causing the anger instead of dwelling on the negative emotions of each other's behavior. A person should also try not to take things personally because it can sometimes cause problems in their relationship and cause them to worry more than necessary about what has happened with their partner. It is also essential for a person to think about their thoughts and make sure they are realistic and make sense when examining them during an angry moment.

Chapter 5

BUILDING AND MAINTAINING A HEALTHY RELATIONSHIP

I t's every couple's dream to have a healthy and happy relationship. But in a world where divorce rates are high, this has become a challenging goal for many. However, it is possible with the right partner and exemplary commitment. There are plenty of ways to build your relationship into a tremendous one-on-one bond that will last forever.

TRUST: THE BEDROCK OF EVERY RELATIONSHIP

Trust is one of the essential things in a relationship. Trust is what keeps a relationship strong and healthy. Without trust, your relationship will deteriorate and fall apart. Trust keeps your eyes wide open when it comes to your partner instead of closing them off from any potential problems or issues that can be happening in the relationship.

Why is trust crucial for healthy relationships?

People in relationships continually try to gain or keep their partner's trust. People also want their partners to feel safe and secure with them, which can make it easier to develop confidence. Trust helps people feel confident when they're speaking with their partners. Relationships are built on the simple principles of trust, respect, and love. Without these three things, couples will have difficulty enjoying a healthy relationship.

To have a healthy relationship, it is essential to trust your partner and listen to them when they're trying to explain their point of view. This means you should stop arguing with your partner if they tell you something you disagree with. Instead, try listening and nodding your head while agreeing to what they are saying. Trust is critical because when you hear and agree with your partner, it makes them feel accepted and not so insecure about what they are saying.

When you put trust between two people, there's a greater chance of the relationship being able to withstand difficult times or personal problems that can arise due to life circumstances. When you trust your partner and don't keep secrets from them, you force them to be completely honest with you. This helps to eliminate all forms of suspicion that can arise in a relationship.

Trust has a crucial role in how well a relationship will perform. You cannot create trust overnight; instead, it should be built over time. Building trust with your partner is critical to truly experiencing the joys of a relationship. When you build trust over time, it can make building intimacy much easier as well.

The role of trust in:

1. Communication

Trust is one of the most vital components for effective, healthy communication. The best communication occurs when both people are on the same page and each partner speaks their mind. Communication should never be complex for your partner because it takes time to build a relationship. The more effort you put into communicating, the quicker trust will be built up in your relationship.

When you can communicate effectively with your partner, they will be able to learn more about you and vice versa. This will make the relationship much more enjoyable When you communicate with your partner, you are more likely to understand and respect your partner's feelings and views. This allows you to feel comfortable enough with them, which will help create intimacy. It will also let them know everything they say is essential when communicating with you. This can help them feel less stressed about the relationship as well.

2. Intimacy

Intimacy is one of the most critical aspects of certain relationships. Intimacy can come from many sources, such as physical contact, conversation, and emotional intimacy. Intimacy is a vital part of every relationship, and plenty of benefits come with it. Intimate relationships provide a safe place for partners to explore their feelings, allowing everyone involved to be more open-minded. Trust is vital in intimate relationships because it will enable partners to be completely comfortable when sharing different parts of themselves. This can help people develop a sense of empathy and understanding as well.

3. Emotional well-being

When you have a healthy relationship, you are more likely to feel better about yourself. When you're in a good relationship, you're less stressed about life, and as a result, your physical health improves as well. The healthier your mental state, the better it is for your well-being. If a person is always blaming their partner or themselves for bad events, they are more likely to be less happy with themselves and start to feel depressed. Trust is crucial to keeping your mind healthy and happy because it helps you believe everything will be okay. Emotional well-being is one of the most important aspects of any relationship because it helps you feel good about yourself. Without it, you're more likely to experience a higher stress level, which will also decrease your social life.

Overall, trust is a crucial aspect that can help any relationship remain strong and vibrant. If you have doubts and insecurities about your partner and what they are saying, it will be hard for your relationship to blossom. When you want to strengthen your relationship, trust should always be built between partners first. Building trust takes time and effort from both people involved, but it can make the overall experience much more worthwhile when done correctly.

Common trust issues in relationships:

Trust issues are a common problem for couples because many of the problems that arise in relationships are trust-based problems. In these situations, one person will feel as though they have been wronged, and the other will feel they need to defend themselves. This can lead to serious arguments and issues between people and their partners. When you're having trust issues with your partner, you do not trust them on any level, which can cause serious issues between couples.

Common trust issues in relationships include:

1. Infidelity

Infidelity is a common problem that can crop up in many relationships. When you're having trust issues with your partner, it's usually because you feel your partner has done something wrong or is doing something that can make you not trust them. Trust is essential to any relationship because communication and intimacy must occur. Without trust, people will have difficulty believing what their partner says and may even start to doubt themselves.

When a person's partner has cheated on them before, they are more likely to cheat on the person again. If a person feels their partner isn't respecting them, it will emotionally damage them. This is because they will feel as though their partner doesn't care about them, making them feel much more insecure and, in turn, more likely to cheat on their partners.

2. Lying

If a person does not trust the information their partner is giving them, they will have trouble believing anything said to them. This also hints at some deeper level of mistrust or another issue altogether. Trust issues grow out of lies because if a person feels as though something has been hidden, there's always a chance that other things are being disguised.

3. Consistency

For a relationship to stay strong, both partners must be consistent in their actions and thoughts. If a person is unsure about their partner or if they are uncertain about something that's been said, that's when trust issues start to arise. Consistency can be difficult because it involves staying on the same page and trusting your partner in what they say. The more consistent you are, you'll likely feel comfortable with your partner. Trust issues may arise in your relationship if you've never been taught how to build trust. If you don't have someone to help you learn how to trust again after a series of bad events, it becomes much harder to regain your trust in that person. Understanding what you feel is essential because it will help you recognize why trust was lost and let you know how to recover it.

Ways to rebuild trust:

Once trust issues arise in a relationship, rebuilding the trust that was initially there would be hard. Building trust takes time and effort, so you must understand that it will not happen overnight. To build trust back up, you need to start small. When you build back trust in your relationship, setting small goals is essential because this will help you prevent disappointment and failure.

You want your partner to understand what steps they can take to rebuild your trust. Taking responsibility for past actions and mistakes will help people regain trust in their partners and rebuild the trust previously lost. Transparency is crucial to regaining your partner's trust because you must be sincere and open about everything. If you're going to lie about one thing, your partner will wonder if you're lying about anything else. Honesty is a crucial factor that helps people to regain trust again, so you want to stay honest with your partner.

Maintaining consistency during all phases of the relationship can help rebuild trust and re-establishing intimacy. If there's no consistency, it will be hard for new ideas to be introduced into the relationship, and you'll lose some of the loving feelings initially there. Trust is fragile, and we tend not to want to invest in someone who has even a small percentage of doubt about what they're saying or doing. Trust is believed to be the most basic and essential of all interpersonal relations. It forms a base for positive relationships with significant economic and social benefits.

SETTING BOUNDARIES: MAKING RELATION HEALTHIER

Boundaries are limits that you set for yourself and your relationships. They're about what you will and won't tolerate in relationships, regardless of whether you've agreed to be in a relationship with someone. Everyone has personal boundaries that determine their willingness to do within a relationship. Setting boundaries is important because it helps you maintain self-respect and respect for others. Setting boundaries can come in many forms, such as saying "no" when they ask for something they don't need or won't get anything out of it. If they want you to spend more time with them, they'll be able to see where they are in your life by checking your calendar and asking you how things are going on certain days. Once you've set boundaries, the other person will be less likely to cross them than if you didn't put any boundaries first.

Importance of setting boundaries in relationships:

Setting boundaries is essential in any relationship because it helps protect and maintain self-respect. You need to set boundaries for your relationships to work as they should because if you feel someone can walk all over you and treat you disrespectfully, this will not be positive for your relationship's integrity. Boundaries are essential within the healthy functioning of relationships, so it's important to set them for you and to set them for your relationships.

You need to research boundaries within your relationship because this will help you be more positive by learning about how boundaries can also benefit you. By setting boundaries within your relationships, you're allowing your partner to feel comfortable enough to make their own decisions, making the relationship much more beneficial for you. You want people to feel safe sharing their thoughts and feelings with you. Still, they need to understand that they would be less likely to have good relationships if they don't respect the relationship and treat others disrespectfully.

How can boundaries prevent conflicts and increase respect and trust?

Boundaries can help prevent or stop conflicts that arise within relationships, which can help regain trust. If you let someone walk all over you, they will take advantage of it and not respect you. It would be best if you made sure that the boundaries are clear and understandable so there won't be any misunderstanding between you. It is essential to learn how limits work within a relationship to stay aware of limitations because this will help you understand how your partner feels about themselves.

Boundaries also increase respect because if people understand that you have limits and that some things are just not okay with them, they'll know how to treat you. This allows them to feel good about themselves because they can feel respected within the relationship. People who appreciate you will be more likely to treat and respect you well. Boundaries help show your partner that there are limits that they need to follow, so they can't take advantage of your kindness and caring behavior.

Tips for setting and healthily communicating boundaries:

1. Being clear and assertive: If a person is vague about their wants, it will be hard to be assertive about their boundaries. People want to feel safe and secure within their relationships, so setting clear boundaries will show them that you can be clear and assertive with your partner. Being assertive helps to build respect within the relationship because when you're able to set clear boundaries for yourself, you'll be a more trustworthy source for your partner. This must be addressed immediately if someone is unclear about what they want from a relationship.

2. Using "I" statements: When setting boundaries, it's important to state things in "I" statements because it shows that the boundaries are about you and only about you. If people use "you" statements, it can be hard for them to feel that what they're doing is called out, so they need to use "I" statements instead. If a person only knows the basics

of setting boundaries within their relationships, then they should use an assertive tone with the other person by stating how something or someone makes them feel. This shows that you're uncomfortable and want them to change their behavior immediately.

3. Respecting the boundaries of others: It's essential to respect them because if you're disrespectful and don't respect someone, that's not respectful toward the other person. It's important to respect people on levels they're at so it doesn't seem like you're treating them like furniture. Respect means showing them how much of a person they are, not that you have absolute control over them.

4. Creating an environment for change: It's important to model healthy boundaries within your relationships by creating a climate for change for yourself and your partner. If one person is very controlling, then it's going to be difficult for you to teach this person how to show respect because they may not understand how they're being disrespectful. You can use different techniques and give them examples to show them how being disrespectful or controlling is wrong.

5. Taking responsibility: At the end of the day, you need to take responsibility for your role in a relationship. This means you must be clear about what you are doing and why you're doing it when setting boundaries.If someone isn't clear about their limitations, then someone else will have to be assertive with that person so they can understand their limits positively.

FORGIVENESS: A KEY TO UNLOCKING YOUR RELATIONSHIP'S FULL POTENTIAL

This is very important in relationships because you don't want to continue to be affected by the negative things a person has done to you. Forgiveness allows you to not hold a grudge against someone who has mistreated you, but this isn't something that comes easily. If it's taken you a while to forgive someone who has hurt or mistreated you, then there's still some work for you to do to forgive them. Forgiveness must be worked at, especially if the other person continues their wrong and doesn't realize what they're doing is harmful.

Forgiving someone who has hurt or treated you poorly takes time, so don't feel as though it's going to happen overnight. What's essential for you to remember is that forgiveness doesn't mean that you trust the other person. People do hurtful things to one another, so if those things happen in your relationship, you need to talk about how the other person can make things better and how they can compensate for the hurtful action.

How can forgiveness benefit relationships?

1. Forgiving someone who has hurt you means that the next time they mistreat you, they won't be able to use that influence to hurt you again because you won't trust them, and you won't feel as though it's okay for them to treat you the way that they have in the past.

2. When someone wrongs another person, it can cause a lot of damage, giving people a lot of stress in their life and making them feel it is their fault that this has happened. If a person forgives another person who has wronged them, then this gives them the ability to let go of that weight and guilt and worry because they know that this isn't something they're responsible for anymore.

3. Forgiving someone who has hurt you means you won't be obsessing over the wrong that they did or how it changed your life. It happened in the past, and there are other things you can focus on now, so you should look forward to the future and focus on what you want to create instead of letting their mistakes negatively affect you.

4. Forgiving someone who has mistreated and hurt you helps to give yourself the freedom to move forward with your life instead of being stuck in the past, which makes it much easier for you. You'll be able to focus on what you want to create and what you want to look forward to instead of being distracted by the wrong someone has done.

5. Forgiveness also helps you move forward because if you're affected by negative things others have done to you, then a lot of energy will be used daily. If someone has hurt or treated you poorly, it might be hard for them to realize this, and it will only make forgiving them even harder.

The role of forgiveness in emotional healing and improved communication:

Forgiveness is essential in a relationship where one person hurts or mistreats the other, but it's also necessary for emotional healing and communication. If you're going to forgive someone who has hurt or mistreated you, then this means that something needs to be fixed and can't be set until they've worked on what they've done.

A person needs to learn how to communicate with one another, so if they can't convey what they want in a helpful way without being hurtful back, they are still stuck in old patterns and need to change how they communicate with one another. Emotional healing lies in forgiveness because you want to move forward and be positive so that you don't continue to feel angry or hurt all the time.

Someone needs to work on their emotions, so if they can't forgive the way they've been hurt, then it means that they are stuck in old habits and trying to break out of those ways can help them to change and grow as a person. It would be best if you learned how to express yourself healthily because being stuck in old forms of communication will be harmful later in your relationship.

If the person is still stuck in old ways of communication and hasn't moved past that, then there won't be any progress made with their emotional healing, which will prevent them from going forward with their lives. Suppose the person you're trying to forgive is struggling with their emotional healing; in that case, they can't progress in their relationship, so a better solution would be for them to work on their emotions instead of holding onto old communication methods.

All of these can help with forgiveness and improving your relationship because they'll allow you to move forward in your life instead of being stuck in old ways, which will prevent you from creating the future that you want to have.

Steps and strategies for practicing forgiveness:

1. Understanding the other person's perspective: If you're having a hard time forgiving someone for what they've done, this is usually because you don't completely under-stand why the person has acted that way toward you. You don't know the other person's

thoughts and the context in which they thought when they did what they did. It would help if you tried to figure out why they did what they did and why it was harmful, and you need to be willing to understand how you contributed to their doing what they did.

2. Focusing on the present and future: You need to think about the present moment and what you want to do in your future life because this will help you release any anger or hurt you have towards the other person. It's common for people who have been hurt to continue to feel hurt all of the time, but when they forgive the other person, they'll be able to move past their anger and hurt. If you want to forgive someone who has hurt or mistreated you, then it's vital not to focus on your anger or where things went wrong in the past because this will make it easier for you both to move forward with your lives.

3. Seeking professional help when needed: When dealing with something as complicated as forgiveness, it's a good idea to seek help from someone who is experienced and can advise you on what to do. If you're stuck in the past and can't forgive another person, you need to change your perspective to move forward. These are some of the steps and strategies you can use when trying to forgive someone who has hurt or mistreated you, and this will help you work through your emotions, so they don't continue to affect your life.

Forgiveness helps you to move forward in life, which means that over time, you'll be able to create the future you want instead of being stuck in old ways which will prevent you from making a better future for yourself.

COMPASSION: A CRUCIAL INGREDIENT TO A HAPPY RELATION-SHIP

Compassion is a rare and beautiful thing that can't be taught. It's an emotion that comes from our inner selves and is defined as the combination of love and empathy. When you're feeling compassion for another, you truly feel their pain and are willing to do whatever it takes so they won't go through the same things you did.

The benefits of compassion in relationships:

Compassion has several benefits, so if you're able to feel empathy for others, then it means that you can rely on your support system in times of need. The significant benefit someone feels when they have a human relationship with another is that they don't have to go through it alone, and there is someone in their life who understands what they're going through and will be there for them.

Compassion is essential because it allows people to feel like they have someone with them through the good times and bad. It's necessary for relationships to be based on compassion because, without this emotion, it'll be challenging to move forward together.

One of the main benefits that someone will feel when they have a compassionate relationship with another is their comfort because they know they can rely on their partner to get through anything. When it comes to relationships, people need to have a foundation they can build on, and trust is a big part of this foundation.

When you're able to feel compassion for another person, it means that you trust them, so if you don't feel like you can trust your partner with anything, then this doesn't build up your relationship and will make you feel less connected.

When someone can feel compassion for others, then this means that they'll be able to help others in need. If you want to be kinder and more compassionate towards others, you need to understand what it feels like in this situation. People who are kind and compassionate are doing this because they want to help others and not do this so that they can look good or gain something from the situation.

The role of compassion in emotional intimacy and understanding:

Compassion is a crucial part of emotional intimacy and understanding. If you want a loving relationship with your partner, you need to understand their feelings when they're going through difficult times. A compassionate relationship means that both people can understand each other, which will allow them to have better feelings towards each other because they'll be able to communicate better.

People with good emotional communication skills need to be able to get the support they need for them and not feel scared or lonely. This can be difficult because you have to let people into your life, which can be scary for many.

People who are compassionate towards others will feel more comfortable around them, which means they'll be able to let their guard down more than before. It's common for people to have their guard up in relationships, and the main reason for this is that they want to protect themselves from getting hurt by their partner.

When you're in a relationship with someone who understands your feelings, it'll be easier for you to let your guard down so you can feel comfortable being yourself around them. To be more compassionate and let your guard down, you must be around others who understand you and want to see the best in you.

Compassion is a powerful emotion that can only come from within, and it's essential for people to feel this emotion whenever they need it. When you're dealing with complex issues, you need someone who understands what you're going through and will help you through these issues.

Tips for practicing compassion in relationships:

There are several ways to practice compassion in your relationships, so if you're interested in being more compassionate and caring toward others, you must know what these methods are and how to use them.

1. Putting yourself in the other person's shoes: You can practice being more compassionate when you take the time to put yourself in the other person's shoes, which means that you understand what they might be thinking or feeling at that moment. If someone is upset with you, it's a good idea for you to try and understand why they feel this way.

2. Practicing empathy: When you're able to put yourself in their shoes and understand what they feel, it's a good idea for you to practice compassion. Doing this will allow you to know how someone feels and how it affects them. You'll be able to try and put yourself in their shoes so that you understand what's going on in their life or why they're feeling the way they are.

3. Being compassionate when things don't go as planned: It's essential for people who want to be more compassionate towards others to know that there will be times when things don't go their way, but this doesn't mean that they shouldn't try anymore. If you want to relate and feel more compassion for others, you must realize that things will not always go how you want them to.

4. Focusing on common humanity: Compassion is a powerful emotion, and when you're able to focus on shared humanity, then it means that you'll have a better understanding of other people, and you'll be able to put yourself in their shoes. This means you'll understand their feelings, allowing you to show compassion towards others when they need it.

5. Letting go of judgment: Many people with a judgmental attitude towards others might not have compassion because they cannot let their guard down and understand what others feel. When you let go of judgment, it'll be easier for you to connect with people and be compassionate toward them.

Compassion is an emotion that comes from within, so if you want others to be compassionate toward you, you need to show compassion whenever your partner struggles with something. If your partner is going through a difficult time, you need to listen and offer support so they know they can trust you with anything and rely on you. Compassion is a powerful emotion, and if you want to deepen your relationships with others and feel more understanding toward them, you need to learn to be more compassionate. Compassion is a good thing because it improves life when someone understands what others are going through. In addition, you need to accept that not everything will go your way, which can be difficult. Working on accepting things is a good way for you to maintain compassion in your life and to be able to feel more understanding towards others.

Chapter 6

ANGER MANAGEMENT DURING TRANSITIONS

A nger can feel like a natural and unavoidable part of relationships. It is not uncommon for one or both people in an intimate connection to lose their temper. It's good that partners can express anger about their needs and wants as long as they do so respectfully. However, anger is common in relationships and serves some essential functions to help the couple succeed in difficult times. Anger can put the other person on notice that something is amiss and motivate them to change course or action.

NAVIGATING RELATIONSHIP TRANSITIONS: HOW TO KEEP YOUR COOL

Relationships are dynamic, unfolding, and evolving, with sometimes unexpected changes that trigger intense emotions and experiences that initially lead to various adverse outcomes. When the transition occurs from one phase to another in the life cycle of a relationship, it can be a stressful and traumatic experience, as people's hopes and expectations are dashed instantly.

Relationship transitions include changes from a couple deciding to end their relationship, from choosing not to continue, from a couple separating after a significant period together, and from deciding to pursue the relationship in a new direction. It can be an intensely challenging process.

A healthy relationship includes several transition processes that allow partners to live with new knowledge, adapt their behaviors accordingly and decide how to move forward. During transition periods, when there is a change in the partnership, couples have difficult choices about how they will maintain or re-establish stability during the transition and look forward to what they want out of the next phase of their lives together. Each partner needs to be able to trust their partner and feel safe during the transition period and have the ability to speak up when things get uncomfortable.

The importance of communication and emotional regulation during changes:

Communication is a fundamental aspect of healthy relationships. For most people, it comes naturally, but it is an area of challenge for some people. People who are not very good at expressing their thoughts and feelings may not see the need to talk about their feelings or thoughts. When this happens, couples can feel stuck in their relationship as they may feel unable to communicate the things that they want out of the relationship. When communication breaks down between partners, it can lead to unresolved issues or angry feelings that drain away the positive energy and happiness that was so much a part of the relationship before.

Communication is essential to help partners understand how they contribute to the everyday stress and unhappiness in the relationship. It allows them to focus on what is important and address the underlying issues that cause conflict in the relationship. When partners understand each other's perspectives, they can work together to solve problems rather than using anger and frustration to deal with challenges.

When managing anger and conflict, communication is vital in helping both partners understand that anger is not always intended to be hurtful or damaging; it can also help get needs fulfilled or change negative behaviors. Understanding your anger is sometimes tricky but knowing how you express anger is even more difficult for couples to grasp.

Communication is essential for helping partners learn new ways of being in the relationship that leads to more positive outcomes. When partners can find the balance between being too strong or weak, critical, or passive, and in control or vulnerable, they develop a better understanding of how to get what they need and stay connected.

Communication serves as a safety net for partners during relationship transitions so that they can rest assured that their feelings and needs will be heard and answered if something happens to scare them now or creates a new upset, such as losing a job or getting into an accident. Engaging in communication about problems during transition helps partners avoid repeating the issue and build positive change that will contribute to more satisfaction in the relationship.

Anger is often displayed during transition periods, as people look at what they have done, how they got there, and how they can make changes to move forward. When couples are not accepting of frustration, anger motivates them to get things done and take action to communicate their feelings more effectively.

Communication is necessary for partners to discuss their needs and the things most important to them in the relationship. For example, a man may not be interested in his partner's feelings about how she thinks he has changed since they married. In turn, he may tune out of discussions about her views on whether they should have children. Even if both are interested in each other's perspectives on these issues, they may not be able to communicate effectively in the relationship.

Relationship transitions can place a heavy burden on couples. Each person's experience of this transition is linked to their emotions and belief system around relationships and needs and wants out of their relationship with each other. Rather than trying to get their needs met through their partner or fighting against the change in the relationship, emotional reactions are often linked to feeling threatened or as if they are losing control over their relationship. As a result, they may act in ways that look selfish and uncaring. This can generate both partners' anger, fear, sadness, and fatigue. Therefore, communication is essential for partners to ease and navigate the transition.

When couples stay in touch with their feelings, they can better deal with relationship transitions and work together toward a positive outcome. Communication is vital in helping partners separate what is important to them so they can have more control over their lives and stand in a relationship together instead of being apart. Communication is vital during times of transition to help partners keep an open mind and make informed decisions about how they want to be connected. Staying open to new ways of being together during transition helps couples recognize that they still have important choices regarding how they want their relationship to operate during transition periods.

MOVING IN TOGETHER

For most couples, the transition from dating to living together is important because it represents a growing commitment to the relationship. While living together may seem like an easy way to settle down and be more comfortable in your relationship, many people find that moving in together can weaken their relationship. For many couples, their first serious relationship is a learning experience because it allows them to get to know each other more intimately and make important decisions about the relationship based on that knowledge. Living together may bring them closer, but it can also lead to couples spending less time discussing essential relationship issues as they are confronting new challenges.

Living together also removes some of the variety in a couple's routine, which can be very exciting in the early stages of a relationship. Over time, they may feel they have less to talk about. The most important thing for a couple moving in together is setting boundaries and expectations. This includes how they want their apartment or house to be as well as how they want their life to be as a couple. Any couples find that once they live together, they realize that some of the things they found so attractive in their partner at first are not so great (for example, messy habits or an obsession with sports).

Setting boundaries allows partners to negotiate these situations before they become a problem.

How do you set boundaries?

- Plan together: Decide what changes each partner needs before moving in and how you will handle those changes.

- Set realistic expectations and goals: Decide what level of involvement you want in each other's lives. Talk about your goals for your relationship and your life together (for example, career, social, family). Discuss things like money management, cleaning, and household chores.

- Be flexible: As with other relationship decisions, it's essential to be flexible when setting boundaries. Make changes so they work for both partners and their situation.

- Communicate your feelings: Don't be afraid to talk about how you feel when things change (for example: feeling more distant, happy, frustrated).

- Set firm time limits: Be open to adjusting as needed and be realistic about what you can reasonably do. If a limit doesn't work, discuss alternatives, like splitting the chore. Decide what's fair and stick with it.

- Be respectful of each other: Don't expect too much from one partner and give less than what you want in return. These dynamics will drain energy and leave both partners feeling like they're giving more than they get.

- Create a schedule: Decide how to split up household duties. This will ensure you're getting your needs met without feeling like one partner is doing all the work.

- Stick with it: Things may not get easier right away. Stick with the boundaries you've set and be honest about how you're feeling and what you need to do to take care of yourself (as well as your relationship).

Transitions can be scary and a little sad, but they are necessary for keeping the life of a relationship alive and full of love, affection, trust, and passion. Keeping these transitions in mind during any season will help to continue the memory of love between two people who mean so much in each other's lives.

When you move in with someone, it is natural for them to think that you will be their friend and do what they want. Learn your boundaries, so you know how to deal with them when they become upset. It's also important not to feel like they're doing what they want because they don't know how to live by their own rules. That will make things worse. Make sure your expectations are clear from the beginning of the relationship. This can be done by using a list of boundaries or discussing them with one another before moving in together.

Household duties and money management are combined, don't expect to live together and have everything sweet like that. Recognize that there will be some conflicts with money and household responsibilities. Work out a plan for finances, chores, and everyday things that must be taken care of. Make sure there's enough money for you and your partner so you won't feel like you're wasting money or debt. When things are out of control financially, it can cause severe problems in the relationship and take away from relationships with other people. Try not to let money issues get in the way of a relationship because they can cause so much stress in a relationship that is already very stressful. Keep the money problems separate and deal with them on their own.

You are dealing with space and privacy issues, moving in with someone is a huge step toward taking your relationship to the next level. It means that you are ready to let go of some of your personal space and independence. Talking with your partner about what boundaries you need and want regarding privacy is essential.

When you move in with someone, there will be times when both partners have friends over and may leave each other out by the wayside or feel like they're not included in any activities because their partner doesn't want them around. If this happens, make sure not to take it personally. Talk about how you want things handled so that each partner feels comfortable with what's happening between you.

It is essential to have some personal time alone. It would help if you had time to be yourself and think about things without being distracted. So, if you have been feeling distanced from your partner lately, try taking time out with friends or doing something yourself. Moving in together can either bring two people closer or drive them apart. It's important to talk about your feelings with one another so that you feel comfortable sharing what you're going through without feeling like you're being judged or hurt in any way.

If you're struggling in your relationship and feel it's going downhill fast, start talking about what you want out of the relationship before it gets worse, and things come to a terrible end. It's essential to have rules for yourself, and you should talk about what you want and need from your partner with them. Don't be afraid to make changes if the boundaries aren't working for you.

MIDLIFE AND EMPTY NEST

When you have children, you're changed forever, and you'll never be the same again. You'll undergo many changes when your children grow up and move on from your home. The empty nest many people go through after their children are grown is very painful for some parents, but it has to be done if you want to live a happy life with or without your partner.

When children leave home and go away to college, it can be a tricky thing to take. You'll be dealing with the fact that they no longer live in the same house as you while they still live under the same roof as their parents. It can be challenging for some parents when their children leave home and face changing their lifestyle because of this significant change. It's nothing that you can control, but it's not something you should let ruin your relationship with your child or break your family apart completely.

It's a good idea to take some time to adjust to this change in your life while also trying not to leave your spouse behind in the dust. They're feeling the same things that you are, so make sure you're getting time together as a couple and working on your relationship. Make sure you have things going on as a couple that will make you happy. You don't have to go out all the time, but it's a good idea to do things that will build up your relationship and make it better. You can take a trip, go out for dinner, or do something simple like take an evening walk together. As long as you're communicating with each other, you can find a way to deal with this change, and it will all be okay in the end. As long as you make time for each other and ensure that both of you are being heard and respected, everything will come out all right in the end.

We are redefining relationships and self-identity, one of the most significant changes you have to deal with is that you'll be redefining yourself and your relationship as a couple. When children leave home, it will change your lives in so many ways, and it will require new skills from both of you if you want to come out on top as a team.

It can be challenging for some people to realize they barely communicate with their spouse. You may not see each other as much or talk as often, but these things don't mean anything if both people feel neglected and taken advantage of by one another. You'll have to redefine your relationship with your children when they start leaving home. You'll be making the most critical decision of your life and will have to face the fact that you'll have to let them go into their adult lives and take care of themselves. This can be hard for some people, but it's a necessary step in your children's growth and they're now becoming adults. When both parents are willing to redefine their relationship with their children, it can make this significant change in their life much easier for everyone involved. You'll still be close as a family while giving each other room to live your lives as individuals.

When children leave home, it will be a big wake-up call for many parents, and it can make them realize how much they've failed as parents. You cannot hide from it and make it go away, but you'll have to deal with it if you want to move on to the next stage in your adult life. It would be best if you addressed any unfulfilled dreams or goals that you may have with your children before they leave home. This is the first time in their life that they will be living out their wildest dreams, so they need someone to help them do this and support them. If you're not discussing your dreams and goals with your spouse, now is the time to do this. It's never too late to accomplish something outstanding and fulfill some of your dreams from when you were younger. You may have to start over in some ways when it comes down to this subject and decide which of you will be fulfilling these dreams for yourselves. You'll also have to decide if one person should move on from their current career or if it will be better for you to stay together as a couple and find a way through this without making drastic changes.

OLD AGE

Old age can be challenging for some people, and it can be scary to think about if you're not expecting this future to happen. There's no reason you shouldn't plan and think about old age as something that will happen in the future. It's something you can take control of and make a lot easier if you want to live longer or live your life with the kind of freedom that older people enjoy. It's essential to plan for old age together and care for yourself when it happens. You may not be able to finish plans for your children if you feel too old, but with enough planning and work, it shouldn't make a difference in your relationship.

As you get older, you will have to deal with many health issues that you won't have to worry about when you're younger. These are the years you'll have to start worrying about things like cancer, heart disease, and other medical conditions. One of the best ways to cope with aging is by ensuring that your mind is as sharp as ever. You should always be reading or going to classes on new subjects if you can do so. Stress can be a killer for your body and brain, so you need to ensure that you're getting enough rest and that your mind is as relaxed as possible.

You may not want to retire entirely if you feel your health is good enough to work at a decent job. As long as you're keeping active and eating right, then there's no reason why you shouldn't be able to go out to another stage in life. If not, then make sure that your spouse gets the same amount of support from your family as they do from their parents during this time of their lives. Health-wise, you will have to take care of your heart and ensure it's always working to the best of its ability. Your heart is one of the critical components of your body, and you'll want to keep it performing at its peak.

If you're in your middle age and you have the health to do so, there are many things that you can do to keep your mind sharp. Exercising and eating right are two things you must do to stay in shape for your old age. You will want to stay as healthy as possible to enjoy your retirement and go on trips during this time. You'll need a good retirement plan set up if you plan on spending a lot of money on vacations from this point on. You may work at the same job until you retire and get everything set up for yourself before you leave work for good.

You may have to adjust to living independently when your children leave home. You may have gotten used to having someone around the house all the time to help with chores and work. When your children go, this leaves a big hole in your lives that you will have to find a way to fill. When it comes down to adjusting after this point of life, it's going to be best if you do things considered average or "typical" for retirees. You'll want something productive and exciting in your life and a change from what you've been doing for years. You may have to move somewhere new to escape the hustle and bustle of your current neighborhood. You can't keep living where you live because it will be difficult for you after your children leave home. You may want to start looking at places that let you do things like water sports and go fishing. Everything is different after they leave the nest, and once they're done with school, they may not be looking for the same things that you are. We are dealing with loss and grief, losing your spouse or children can be a tough time in your life. You must accept the loss and carry on without their presence, but this is never easy. When your children leave home, there's a lot of pain that they'll feel, making it even harder for you to handle.

When it comes down to dealing with the loss of a spouse or child, this is something you'll never get over, no matter how much time passes. You can do things while they're gone, such as staying active and fighting against loneliness, but there will always be that hole inside you where they once lived. You'll want to do things they love while they're gone, but there comes a time when you can't stand to live in the same place you lived with them. This cannot be easy, but you must do it to move on with your life. It's best to keep busy and stay active during this time of your life because it will make it easier for you.

What you choose to do during these different stages of your life is up to you, but it's essential for both of you, as a couple or family unit, to put some time aside for planning and discussing what the future will look like when each of those stages comes around.

When it comes down to planning for your end-of-life care, this is something that you're going to have to discuss with your family while you're still alive. You'll have a better idea if they are willing to take care of you when the time comes and will want to give them as much information as possible so that they'll know how to handle things from this point on. It would help if you also were prepared for the possibility that your spouse will not make it through this last stage of their life. If this happens, you'll want to ensure that you've taken care of your family's needs so that everything will go smoothly for them after you pass away.

General Anger Management Techniques

When it comes down to dealing with anger and frustration, it's best that you first attempt to deal with it when you're alone. If you walk up to your spouse and start yelling at them while they're working on something and get into an argument with them, you will find a reason to blame each other and wind up having a bad day.

It's better to take the time out and go for a brisk walk around the neighborhood if you need to release some built-up frustration or anger before speaking with your spouse. This will leave the stress away from your relationship, which can help settle things before they escalate into full-blown verbal assault.

Identifying triggers and warning signs:

Many things can be done regarding identifying what triggers your anger and how you deal with it. If someone makes an off-hand comment that rubs you the wrong way, perhaps ignore them or tell yourself to let these comments roll off of your back. This will help you not take these comments so seriously and help lessen the stress when they're made.

Some triggers and warning signs of anger include sweaty palms, a rapid heartbeat, and heavy breathing. Your heartbeat will speed up when you're angry, which can lead to other issues if you don't take the time to calm down.

When you face these warning signs, it's best to take the time out somewhere to relax your body before going back home and dealing with problems. If you're in a place with no room for escape, it's best to leave the area as quickly as possible. You'll want to get away from everyone else so that no one will see how out of control your anger is.

Once you know what triggers your anger and when to expect them, then you'll be ready to control it when they do show up. The more that you work with this, the more in control of yourself you will be. You'll have a better chance at controlling things if you know what will set you off before it happens.

When it comes down to warning signs indicating that your anger is starting to build, they will be entirely different for different people. Some people may feel in the pit of their stomach, while others might start sweating or have trouble focusing on their work, and movements become slower.

Communication and active listening:

When it comes down to healthy communication and active listening, this is something that you will have to work on for the rest of your life. There are times when you'll have your say, and there will be times when the other person will want to let their feelings out and express them. If these things happen, you must listen and try not to interrupt or judge their actions.

When you wind up in a fight with your spouse, it's best to find a quiet place to argue without the kids or anyone else listening. If you insist on fighting these things at home, nothing will get resolved, and you will be left with a ruined relationship.

When it comes to healthy communication, you must acknowledge what the other person has said through active listening. This means you take the time to hear them and believe what they're saying before giving your side. This will show your partner that you care more about the relationship than you do yourself and will help prevent arguments from getting so out of hand.

When it comes to active listening, you should be wholly committed to the other person's point of view. Regardless of whether or not it's something that you agree with, if they're trying to let you know how they feel, then you can't be rude and interrupt them to get your way.

If your spouse gets upset with this, they will stop trying to explain their feelings once they realize their message is being ignored. If this happens while they can still control their emotions, the situation might get better over time.

Just because you're angry does not mean you're 100% correct and should try to get your way at all costs. If you do this and end up with your spouse hating you for it in the long run, there will be no hope of repairing the relationship.

If this happens, both people should sit down and talk things out instead of letting their feelings build up. This will prevent damage from being done while they can still control themselves and work through the issues that are causing them stress.

Time-outs and self-care:

When it comes to time-outs and self-care, this should be a part of everyone's daily routine instead of waiting for the moment when you're in such emotional pain that you need to do something about it, when you're unable to tell your partner what's wrong and why they are naturally going to be concerned.

You'll want to start taking breaks when they occur to control your emotions. Talking with someone who knows how you feel and deal with stress can be a way for you to take a break and get your emotional needs met without worrying too much about the repercussions.

When it comes down to taking breaks, you want to find a quiet place where you won't be disturbed by people and can be completely alone. There will be times when you're so angry that even the people around you will make your anger worse, so if you can't get away right then, try to do it at some point in the future.

Seeking professional help if needed:

When it comes down to seeking professional help if needed, this is something that you should only do if things get out of hand. When you're dealing with anger issues, and it's starting to affect other areas of your life, you should seek help. When you go in for an appointment, they will want to know what's causing the stress in your life and if there are any warning signs that your anger might worsen. If these warning signs include violence and threats, then they will want to be able to help you deal with these issues before they get out of control.

A certified mental health professional will be the best resource for you when it comes to helping with your anger. This means you will look into everything from counseling and medication to group and therapy sessions.

Chapter 7

CONCLUSION

B uilding a better relationship through conflict and anger management is an on-going, albeit challenging, process. But the benefits are often worth it in the end. The most important thing is to understand one another's point of view before trying anything else; that means listening without interjecting or going ahead with an action plan right away.

Anger can be so destructive that we need a way to harness its power while keeping it under control. Recognizing the warning signs of an impending anger outburst is one way to positively channel the energy around us. Sometimes, however, it can be challenging to maintain control over our feelings. If you need help with managing and dealing with anger, there are many helpful tools you can turn to.

You need to know that telling your partner how you feel is okay. The key is to be honest without being critical or attacking the other person. Remember, the goal is to heal any existing wounds in your relationship so that you can communicate more effectively and bring out the best in each other.

One of the reasons we lose control over our emotions is that we don't know how to han-dle them properly. When trying to avoid a conflict resolution situation, it's important to remember that remaining calm and focused will always be far more effective than losing your temper. This doesn't mean we shouldn't try to communicate our feelings with our partners; we should express them constructively and positively rather than accusingly. We should always set aside our emotions to look at the situation rationally.

These are all strategies you can use to help you control your feelings when they get the best of you. Try implementing any or all of these strategies in your relationships and see how they enable you better manage yourself and your emotions.

The only way to avoid a problem during an argument is not to have one at all. If both members of the couple can keep from saying something hurtful, this will save both members from unnecessary drama and stress. Another way to avoid arguments is to ensure you begin the conversation in a normal tone. If you are angry or frustrated, it may be hard to clearly explain what you are feeling. Your partner may also be on edge and have trouble hearing what you say.

It's also important to try not to begin an argument over something, then go on a different topic and then come back around. When this happens, they are often referred to as "going round and round." It's best to stay on one topic and get everything out at once. When it becomes necessary for the couple to talk about an issue, they should sit down together in a quiet place where they can talk without distractions.

It's important to know that anger is not just one emotion — it's a range of emotions, from frustration to fury. Sometimes anger can be justified, but often the problem with anger is that it feels like the only emotion we're feeling. Anger can make us feel like there's no other option but to yell and curse. And yet, there are so many ways of handling our anger besides lashing out. Your relationship can survive an argument or two —if you know what you're doing when you argue with each other, it will mean that your relationship can grow stronger and become healthier instead. Working with a certified therapist who fights anger is always a good idea. In the long run, that will be much more helpful than getting angry. Responding to anger can be a bad idea in your relationship. One thing to do is to ignore the offending partner and walk away for a couple of minutes to cool off.

Beginnings are usually essential, so tell your significant other what you want. Try not to leave them guessing, as it's more likely that both of you will get frustrated as time goes on if you're on a wild goose chase. This method may take some time, but it can prevent unnecessary conflicts.

Keep in mind that communication is vital. One partner needs to speak up and ask their significant other questions when they have something they need answers to. Another key is ensuring the proper tone is used when asking these questions or speaking to them. This can help prevent unnecessary arguments as well.

Once you've gotten over your anger issue and can live a relatively everyday life again, try practicing gratitude. This skill can benefit your life, even if it initially seems trivial. It will allow you to focus on the good things around you and make them stand out from all the negativity in your life. It's also possible for you to develop a habit of practicing gratitude; just set aside a few minutes every day to count your blessings.

Controlling your emotions is vital to having a good relationship. However, if you get angry often, it's essential to understand how to channel that negative energy in a way that won't hurt anyone. To get rid of your anger once and for all, you must replace it with something else. One great way of doing so is by meditating. All you have to do is sit in a quiet place where there are no distractions, concentrate on breathing, and clear your mind.

Once you're done meditating, try doing some yoga exercises. You can also take up some self-improvement activities that will help you learn how to control your emotions. You don't have to stay stuck in one place all the time; if you know your activity, you can do things outside your comfort zone.

If you are willing to put in the time, effort, and energy that this book requires, I will say that you will have a healthier relationship with your partner instead of dealing with all the negative emotions you're experiencing. I hope you learned how to eliminate any anger in your life just by picking up this book.

I hope this book showed you how to keep your relationship alive and well. I hope it gave you tools to talk about your anger and deal with conflicts constructively and give you a new perspective on the issues in your relationship. The book has excellent tips on how you can adjust your mindset. You need to change your thinking to start giving love without expecting anything.

Printed in Great Britain
by Amazon